T0246658

PRAISE FOR A SPELL A DAY

"In *A Spell a Day*, Tree Carr brings us a treasure trove of smart, modern spells that will inspire and empower any reader. Taking an ingenious and innovative turn, Tree seamlessly blends modern sensibilities with the age-old practice of spell casting for all skill levels to explore. This well-rounded and masterfully presented collection of innovative spell work is an excellent addition to anyone's magical library."
Dee Norman, author of *Burn a Black Candle*

"A self-care practice should be accessible to everyone: Tree created this book to guide you into your own magical exploration of the elements as mirrors of parts of yourself. A practical and playful book for bringing more magic to your everyday life."
Bel Senlle, author of *Clarity Tarot*

"A delightful romp through many types of spellcraft curated by the knowledgeable and excellent Tree Carr. *A Spell A Day* provides an accessible range of practices, including modern digital magic, without requiring readers to buy a million bits of paraphernalia to get started. This approachable grimoire includes a straightforward introduction to occult work and a panoply of techniques for readers to try. Recommended."
Julian Vayne, occultist, writer and psychonaut

"This is a book of powerful wisdom. I adore Tree Carr. She brilliantly transforms deep esoteric teachings into accessible practices that yield results. All with a love and compassion that can truly be felt."
Remington Donovan, author of *Numerology: A Beginner's Guide to the Spiritual Meaning of Numbers*

Tree Carr

A SPELL A DAY

365 EASY SPELLS, RITUALS AND MAGIC FOR EVERY DAY

THIS BOOK IS DEDICATED TO ANDREW WEATHERALL

A Spell a Day
Tree Carr

First published in the UK and USA in 2023 by Watkins, an imprint of Watkins Media Limited
Unit 11, Shepperton House,
83–93 Shepperton Road
London N1 3DF

enquiries@watkinspublishing.com

Commissioning Editor: Ella Chappell
Assistant Editor: Brittany Willis
Copyeditor: Elizabeth Kim
Proofreader: Victoria Godden
Head of Design: Karen Smith
Designer: Glen Wilkins
Design Concept: Alice Claire Coleman
Production: Uzma Taj

A CIP record for this book is available from the British Library

ISBN: 978-1-78678-740-8 (Hardback)
ISBN: 978-1-78678-741-5 (eBook)

10 9 8 7 6 5 4 3 2 1

Printed in China

www.watkinspublishing.com

Publisher's note
The spells in this book should not replace any medical, psychological or practical interventions and does not claim to be an ultimate authority that can and will change the destiny of your life. This book cannot guarantee that the spells cast will produce the desired results. The herbs used in this book are at your own risk. Always conduct an allergy test before use. Pregnant women should entirely avoid ingesting any of the herbs mentioned in this book. Consult your GP if you are unsure about any of the herbs before ingesting.

FSC
www.fsc.org
MIX
Paper | Supporting responsible forestry
FSC® C005748

CONTENTS

INTRODUCTION

Hello, magical being! Welcome to your journey through 365 spells. Each spell is handcrafted and centred around elemental magic. With more than 25 years of work in the magical realm, I will be guiding your craft, using a mix of natural materials, mindfulness, creativity and modern technology – yes, our phones can be magical tools! The spells in this book are held in the spirit of creativity and curiosity and are an invitation to explore the world around you as well as within you. These spells are like mini adventures that will make your mundane day to day more magical! I hope this book helps manifest your intentions and connects you with your inner magic.

✳ HOW TO USE THIS BOOK

Before we start on our journey of discovering 365 spells, I first want to provide a brief overview on spellcraft – from etiquette to the different laws – and show you how to create the best environment for your spellwork. For those starting from scratch, or in need of a refresher, I will run through energy cleansing and casting circles. It is important that you open a circle before you start any spell, so please consult this section before beginning your spellwork. It is also important that you express gratitude to the Universe at the end of every spell, and then close your circle.

There are many ways to choose which spell to cast:

★ **Set intentions:** Your will and intentions will bring you to the page that most suits your needs. This act of intention will help fuel your magic making.

★ **Chronologically:** There is a spell for every day of the year, so you can move through the book chronologically, focusing on one spell every day for the next 365 days.

★ **Synchronicity:** Pay attention to the celestial events and magical dates. Check which date the full moon or new moon falls on, and when certain astrological events will happen, using an app or website like moonphases.co.uk, and select the spell based on the next celestial event.

★ **Try bibliomancy:** Try the ancient divinatory art of bibliomancy. Let the pages of this book flick through your fingers, at random, and then open at a page. Perhaps your intuition has guided you toward the spell you need right now.

An integral foundation of magical practice is to know thyself and to be in good working order. For this reason, I recommend that you keep a journal throughout your spellcraft journey as a great way to check in with yourself. You should also create time and space for solitude and meditation. This can be done by your altar or in a soothing bath.

THINGS TO KNOW BEFORE
CASTING THE SPELLS

RECITE YOUR INTENTION

Each spell will require you to recite some words in order to present your intentions to the Universe. These words can be spoken aloud, thought internally or written down. This is a personal choice I will leave with you.

SIGILS

A lot of the spells will ask you to create a sigil – either with pen and paper or on your phone so you can send it to yourself. If you are creating a physical sigil, use your initials and add the symbols each spell requires between the two letters. You can find what each symbol looks like on the page opposite. If you are creating a digital sigil, use emojis to create each symbol. One of the common sigils is the symbol for protection, which looks like this: 👁📱👁

EASY SPELLS

It is possible to perform some of the spells on the go. I have signposted these spells using this symbol: Ⓔ These spells will require you to have limited resources to hand.

SYMBOLS GUIDE

ELEMENTS

△	△	▽	▽	✳
AIR	FIRE	WATER	EARTH	SPIRIT

MOONS AND SUN

●	○	☉
NEW MOON	FULL MOON	SUN

ZODIAC SIGNS

♈︎	♋︎	♎︎	♑︎
ARIES	CANCER	LIBRA	CAPRICORN
♉︎	♌︎	♏︎	♒︎
TAURUS	LEO	SCORPIO	AQUARIUS
♊︎	♍︎	♐︎	♓︎
GEMINI	VIRGO	SAGITTARIUS	PISCES

PLANETS

♀	☿	♂	♆
VENUS	MERCURY	MARS	NEPTUNE
♅	♃	♄	♇
URANUS	JUPITER	SATURN	PLUTO

PART I

A BRIEF HISTORY OF SPELLCRAFT

WHAT ARE SPELLS?

A spell is like a magical conversation between you and the Universe, offering a spiritual way for you to express your deepest desires and manifest them. The intention of spells is to influence events or bring about a desired effect, by using occult forces through will and intention. You can speak, think or write them down, and strengthen your will with ritual and material objects. A spell has two defined stages: in the first, an intention is set (there is a gathering of power), while the second stage focuses on releasing gathered power – action is taken through casting. Spells should be in alignment with your higher good. There is one key rule: harm none.

SPELLCRAFT ETIQUETTE

Etiquette is important and should be taken seriously. Let consideration, honesty and respect – with the intention of doing no harm – guide your spellcasting practice. Here are some things to consider before you begin.

GOOD INTENTIONS

Always ask yourself why you are casting a spell, and whether it is for the higher good of all concerned. Spellcrafting should not be used to control, manipulate or influence others. Only cast a spell for another person if they have consented, and avoid imposing your beliefs on other people.

PRIVACY

Spellcraft should be private. The old saying, "If you tell a wish, it won't come true" has some truth behind it. The thoughts and emotions of others might interfere with the spell's power and potency.

ENERGY CLEANSING

Don't forget to cleanse your personal energy, and the energy of the space that you are in. It will keep you and others protected from psychic attack or from absorbing negative energy. For more guidance, see page 19.

ENVIRONMENT

If you are spellcrafting outside in nature, leave the area the way you found it. Use materials and tools that do not harm the natural environment. Practise fire safety! If you are using candles, never leave them unattended and incorporate the extinguishing of the candle into your ritual.

THE FIVE ELEMENTS

Around 450 BC, the Ancient Greeks identified four elements: air, fire, water and earth. The mystical fifth element of aether (spirit) was later introduced by Aristotle in the 4th century BC, by way of his teacher Plato. It was thought that aether was responsible for creating the Universe and celestial spheres.

ELEMENTAL MAGIC

The natural elements still play an important role in magical practice. This book is structured around elemental magic; the 365 spells are separated into each of the five elements. Within all five sections, you will find moonology Spells, Solar Return Spells and Special Events Spells, before moving to spells that can be used any time of the year. You will learn how to connect to the energy of each element and then channel that energy into your spells.

So, let's get to know the elements!

WHICH ELEMENT DO YOU RELATE TO?

We carry all the elements within us, but we might connect to some more than others. Identifying and learning about the element most dominant within you helps with spellcasting – it can also indicate where you need to become more energetically balanced. Here are some examples of qualities associated with different elements:

- △ **Air:** Intellectual, spiritual, communicative, free-spirited
- △ **Fire:** Action-orientated, passionate, temperamental, competitive
- ▽ **Water:** Intuitive, healing, creative, emotional
- ▽ **Earth:** Loyal, pragmatic, down to earth, nurturing
- ⊕ **Spirit:** Bridge between physical and spiritual, omnipresent, omniscience and omnipotent

PART II

GETTING
STARTED

CREATING SACRED SPACE FOR YOUR SPELLWORK

Claiming a designated area in your home for spellcasting ensures your privacy, but also renders that space sacred. Try to find a spot that is your own. It could be a section in a room, or a private room or garden, if you have that luxury. The place should intuitively make you feel good and calm.

HOW TO CLEANSE YOUR SPACE

Once you have chosen your space, it is time to cleanse it and ensure you are spellcasting in the best energetic climate. To cleanse a space, buy or make a herb bundle. Remember that some cleansing tools are sacred to indigenous cultures and are overharvested for a consumer's market, such as white sage and Palo Santo. A good rule of thumb is to look to your own indigenous herbs. For example, I'm of Celtic ancestry and I use vervain and mugwort. To cleanse your space:

1. Light your herb bundle and allow for the smoke to fill the room.
2. Walk around the space directing the smoke to each corner of the room.
3. With your intention and with present awareness, recite:

"Through the power of intention and with the sacred plant ally of [name the plant], I clear this space of any psychic dissonance, energetic imprints or blocks and any energy that is not in alignment with the higher good. I claim this space for magic, healing, inspiration, clarity and connection to spirit. So may it be."

HOW TO OPEN YOUR SPACE

Now that you have a designated and cleansed sacred space, you are ready to move into the practice of opening up space before your rituals take place. This process includes centring, grounding and shielding. You must first prepare yourself energetically through meditation. This will slow down the chatter of your mind and bring you into the present moment.

CENTRING

Once you are in a meditative state of awareness, you will be able to sense the subtle energies or sensations in your body. The process of centring is the foundation of energy work and means coming back to your source energy. This will be helpful when you begin to understand how to direct energy toward your intentions in spells. To centre yourself:

1. Hold the palms of your hands in prayer position, about an inch apart, and focus your awareness on your fingertips.
2. Observe any sensations arising – you may notice tingling or pins and needles in your fingers.
3. Bring your awareness into the palms of your hands and observe any sensations – you may notice tangible energy here too.
4. Focus your awareness on the core of your energy (solar plexus or heart chakra).
5. Connect the moving energy through your body back to your core.

GROUNDING

After centring, don't forget grounding, which is a way of balancing the energy within us or around us. While doing this, you may choose to hold on to an earthing object, such as smoky quartz, an earthing stone or wood. To ground, you will need to:

1. Close your eyes.
2. Focus your awareness on the sensations around your contact points with the earth.
3. Visualize the earth's energy moving up into the soles of your feet.
4. Pull this energy up your body, through the top of your head.

SHIELDING

Shielding is a kind of protection; it entails creating an energy barrier around yourself so that you can do your spellwork without interference from unwanted and unhelpful energies. To shield, you will need to:

1. Close your eyes.
2. Breathe in deeply through the nose and out through the mouth.
3. Focus your awareness on the core of your energy (solar plexus or heart chakra).
4. Connect to your source energy with love and gratitude.
5. Start expanding your source energy outward from your body.
6. Direct your energy around you to form a bubble.

Now your space is ready for your spellwork to begin.

HOW TO CREATE YOUR ALTAR

You've chosen and cleansed a place to do magic, but it's missing one thing: your altar. Some people don't use one and some do – this is a personal choice so I will leave it up to you.

CHOOSE YOUR OBJECTS

Gather any magical tools in your arsenal, such as cleansing tools, candles, Tarot cards or your dream journal. Then it is time to choose your personal items, such as heirlooms, your favourite herbs and things gathered from nature like pinecones, acorns and branches (don't take more than you need).

Some of the objects on your altar should correlate to elements, to draw in elemental power. Some examples are:

★ **Air:** Feathers, fans, incense, images of birds or butterflies
★ **Fire:** Candles, fiery stones, images of dragons or salamanders
★ **Water:** A bowl or cup of water, shells, images of dolphins or mermaids
★ **Earth:** Soil, plants, wood, stones, salt, images of gnomes or elves
★ **Spirit:** Objects that represent spirit guides, ancestors, goddesses, angels (or images of these)

Once you have chosen the objects for your altar, you will need to cleanse them. As we did when cleansing your space, use your cleansing tool (such as a herb bundle) and speak these words:

"I cleanse and claim this object for my spellwork.
May it be used for the higher good. So may it be."

ACTIVATE YOUR ALTAR

Activate your altar by lighting the candles, incense or burning any resins that you have in your cauldron and speaking words of intention:

"I activate this altar to be a place where I do my magical work in alignment with the higher good. So may it be."

Your altar is now complete!

MAINTAIN YOUR ALTAR

But wait! It doesn't stop here! Keep your altar maintained and activated by:

★ Replacing flowers
★ Watering plants
★ Replacing candles
★ Cleaning the cauldron
★ Dusting and cleaning

HOW TO CAST AND CLOSE A CIRCLE

A circle is a designated space created to contain energy for ritual, keeping your working space safe and energetically charged. It is important to remember to cast a circle before you cast any of the spells in this book!

✕ CIRCLE OF LIGHT

Cast an energetic circle by calling in light to fall all around you and the area where you are working through a combination of hand gestures and words. Once you have drawn the circle, say these words:

"I call in light and cast a circle of light to fall all around me, keeping me safe, protected and contained throughout this ritual. So may it be."

DRAWING THE CIRCLE ◊°

A circle can also be physically cast by drawing it on the floor. Using chalk, salt or flour, draw your circle around you and the ritualistic objects you are using. Once your circle is cast, you shouldn't leave it until you have finished your spell.

CONNECT YOUR CIRCLE WITH THE ELEMENTS

In modern Pagan Witchcraft, elements are associated with four directions on a compass. Your circle should be oriented to the four cardinal points: earth to the north, air to the east, fire to the south, and water to the west. Sit or stand in your magic circle, orient yourself – or a hand or wand – toward the first direction, and call it in verbally, using the formula:

> *"I call the spirit of the [direction] into this circle,*
> *invoking the element of [element]."*

Move through all the cardinal points as you call in the four directions. Focus on the energy that each element brings with it into your circle. You may also want to call in the elusive spirit element from above.

CLOSING A CIRCLE

After completing your spellwork, you will need to close your circle. Thank the four directions and close the circle by casting in reverse. Say these words:

> *"I now close this circle and portal, sealing it up and settling*
> *the energy here in this space. So may it be."*

If you physically cast your circle, dismantle it by erasing the chalk, dismantling stones, etc.

PREPARING YOUR TOOLKIT

You don't need to have to splurge on gear to cast spells. You hold magic within you. However, when starting out, some basic tools serve as extensions of your will and help you focus. Cleanse and claim them as your magical tools (see page 19).

Here is a list of everyday tools useful in spellcrafting, many of which you may find in your cupboards or garden:

★ Candles, lighter or matches
★ A pen and paper
★ Your phone
★ Herbs: each spell will dictate which ones it needs
★ Other ingredients include salt, flour and nuts
★ A feather or fan
★ A pestle and mortar (for grinding and blending herbs)
★ A jar (recycle your old jam jars!)
★ Yarn, string, ribbon or cord
★ Kitchen utensils, including a plate, bowl and knife

And here are a few items that you might find useful to add to a shopping list:

★ A fireproof cauldron (most fire spells will need one!)
★ Charcoal discs
★ Tarot cards: the Rider–Waite–Smith deck
★ A soldering kit
★ Small bags/pouches/sachets

✳ HERBS

Many of the spells in this book require herbs. Opt for local herbs to which you have a cultural link. For herbs from other cultures, learn about their origin. Avoid herbs altogether if your use harms the community that uses them ceremonially or endangers the plant. For example, white sage is sacred to Native American culture and is in short supply as a consequence of cultural appropriation and commodification, which means Native Americans find it difficult to source to use in their sacred practice.

Some spells will list multiple herbs. If you only have one herb, not to worry! You can choose to use just one or, if you have more than one, you can make a blend by grinding your chosen herbs with your pestle and mortar. Spells that involve making tea will, however, require specific herbs.

OFFERINGS ✕

Some spells require offerings. When out in nature, offerings should be biodegradable, and noninvasive to the habitat. For example, seed and nut offerings should be safe for the local area. Before you bring an offering out into a natural habitat, research what local flora and fauna need.

◊ CRYSTALS

Crystals are naturally found in the earth and are extracted by mining. This process has environmental impacts and potentially harms labourers. Crystals can also be expensive! To reduce your impact, avoid hoarding crystals, and buy second-hand crystals, crystal kits, or purchase from companies like Crystal Clear™, which promotes mine-to-market crystals with a social conscience.

Some of the spells will ask you to lay out your crystals in a crystal grid. A crystal grid is the intentional arrangement and placement of crystals and/or stones to manifest a specific result.

PART III

SPELLS AND RITUALS

AIR
SPELLS

Work with the elemental magic of air in the spring for all things related to communication, technology, ideas, innovations, clarity, downloads, knowledge, numbers, music, learning, bringing insight, purification, initiation and activation. In each of the air spells, is it important to envision the energy of the air moving through you, contributing its power to your intentions.

NEW MOON IN LIBRA

The new moon in Libra is a powerful time to invite balance, harmony and truth into your life.

You will need:

- ★ A candle
- ★ A pen and paper
- ★ A jar
- ★ Lemongrass
- ★ A feather
- ★ A crystal: amber
- ★ Incense
- ★ A Tarot card: Justice

THE SPELL

1. Light the candle.
2. Focus on your intention and visualize it coming into being.
3. Write your intention on a piece of paper.
4. Fold the paper and mark it with the symbols for the new moon, Libra and Venus.
5. Prepare your spell jar by adding the sigil, lemongrass, feather, crystal and smoke from the incense. Put a lid on the jar to trap the smoke.
6. Hold the jar in your hands and close your eyes.
7. Recite:
   "By the power of the new moon in Libra and the element of air, I manifest my intention. So may it be."
8. Place your sigil spell jar on your altar, with the Justice card on top.
9. Blow out the candle.

NEW MOON IN AQUARIUS

The new moon in Aquarius is a powerful time to invite innovation, revolution and community into your life.

You will need:

★ A candle
★ A pen and paper
★ A jar
★ Comfrey
★ A feather
★ A crystal: lazurite
★ Incense
★ A Tarot card:
  the Star

THE SPELL

1. Light the candle.
2. Focus on your intention and visualize it coming into being.
3. Write your intention on a piece of paper.
4. Fold the paper and mark it with the symbols for the new moon, Aquarius and Uranus.
5. Prepare your spell jar by adding the sigil, herb, feather, crystal and smoke from the incense. Put a lid on the jar to trap the smoke.
6. Hold the jar in your hands and close your eyes.
7. Recite:
   "By the power of the new moon in Aquarius and the element of air, I manifest my intention. So may it be."
8. Place your sigil spell jar on your altar, with the Star card on top.
9. Blow out the candle.

NEW MOON IN GEMINI

The new moon in Gemini is a powerful time to invite learning, adaptability and socializing into your life.

You will need:

★ A candle
★ A pen and paper
★ A jar
★ Dill
★ A feather
★ A crystal: moonstone
★ Incense
★ A Tarot card: the Lovers

THE SPELL

1. Light the candle.
2. Focus on your intention and visualize it coming into being.
3. Write your intention on a piece of paper.
4. Fold the paper and mark it with the symbols for the new moon, Gemini and Mercury.
5. Prepare your spell jar by adding the sigil, herb, feather, crystal and smoke from the incense. Put a lid on the jar to trap the smoke.
6. Hold the jar in your hands and close your eyes.
7. Recite:
   "By the power of the new moon in Gemini and the element of air, I manifest my intention. So may it be."
8. Place your sigil spell jar on your altar, with the Lovers card on top.
9. Blow out the candle.

FULL MOON IN LIBRA

The full moon in Libra is a powerful time to let go of indecisiveness, impatience and victimization.

You will need:

★ A candle
★ A crystal: black obsidian
★ Incense
★ A fan or feather

THE SPELL

1. Light the candle.
2. Place the crystal in front of the candle.
3. Hold the incense in your hand.
4. Close your eyes and focus on any feelings of indecisiveness, impatience or victimization that you want to let go of.
5. Envision your emotional release travelling into the incense stick.
6. Light the incense and let the smoke move in front of you.
7. Recite:
   "By the power of the full moon in Libra and the element of air I blow away [name the issue] and I set myself free. So may it be."
8. Blow the smoke of the incense away from you.
9. Open a window and move the smoke outside with a fan or feather.
10. Blow out the candle.

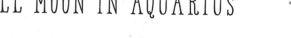

FULL MOON IN AQUARIUS

The full moon in Aquarius is a powerful time to let go of anger, pessimism and judgement.

You will need:

★ A candle
★ A crystal: black obsidian
★ Incense
★ A fan or feather

THE SPELL

1. Light the candle.
2. Place the crystal in front of the candle.
3. Hold the incense in your hand.
4. Close your eyes and focus on any feelings of anger, pessimism or judgement you want to remove from your life.
5. Envision your emotional release travelling into the incense stick.
6. Light the incense and let the smoke move in front of you.
7. Recite:
   "By the power of the full moon in Aquarius and the element of air I blow away [name the issue] and I set myself free. So may it be."
8. Blow the smoke of the incense away from you.
9. Open a window and move the smoke outside with a fan or feather.
10. Blow out the candle.

FULL MOON IN GEMINI

The full moon in Gemini is a powerful time to let go of moodiness, confusion and anxiety.

You will need:

- ★ A candle
- ★ A crystal: black obsidian
- ★ Incense
- ★ A fan or feather

THE SPELL

1. Light the candle.
2. Place the crystal in front of the candle.
3. Hold the incense in your hand.
4. Close your eyes and focus on any moodiness, confusion or anxiety you want to release.
5. Envision your emotional release travelling into the incense stick.
6. Light the incense and let the smoke move in front of you.
7. Recite:
   "By the power of the full moon in Gemini and the element of air I blow away [name the issue] and I set myself free. So may it be."
8. Blow the smoke of the incense away from you.
9. Open a window and move the smoke outside with a fan or feather.
10. Blow out the candle.

SOLAR RETURN LIBRA

Happy Birthday, Libra! Birthdays hold potent energy for spellwork. It's time to honour the return of the sun to the natal chart position that you were born in. Cast this spell for creating harmonious balance with clear decision-making for the year ahead.

You will need:

★ A candle
★ A pen and paper
★ A jar
★ Lemongrass
★ A feather
★ A crystal: amber
★ Incense
★ Tarot cards

THE SPELL

1. Light the candle.
2. Close your eyes and connect with your intention.
3. Write your birthday wish on a piece of paper.
4. Fold the paper and mark it with the symbols of the sun, Libra and Venus.
5. Prepare your spell jar by adding the sigil, herb, feather, crystal and smoke from the incense. Put a lid on the jar to trap the smoke.
6. Hold the jar in your hands and close your eyes.
7. Recite:
   "I honour the sun and my life on this day of my solar return. I call on the element of air. Move quickly to activate my purpose and manifest my wishes this coming year. So may it be."
8. Pull a Tarot card for your year ahead.
9. Place your sigil spell jar on your altar alongside the Tarot card.
10. Blow out the candle.

SOLAR RETURN AQUARIUS

Happy Birthday, Aquarius! Birthdays hold potent energy for spellwork. It's time to honour the return of the sun to the natal chart position that you were born in. Cast this spell to revolutionize your year ahead.

You will need:

- ★ A candle
- ★ A pen and paper
- ★ A jar
- ★ Comfrey
- ★ A feather
- ★ A crystal: lazurite
- ★ Incense
- ★ Tarot cards

THE SPELL

1. Light the candle.
2. Close your eyes and connect to your intention.
3. Write your birthday wish on a piece of paper.
4. Fold the paper and mark it with the symbols of the sun, Aquarius and Uranus.
5. Prepare your spell jar by adding the sigil, herb, feather, crystal and smoke from the incense. Put a lid on the jar to trap the smoke.
6. Hold the jar in your hands and close your eyes.
7. Recite:
   "I honour the sun and my life on this day of my solar return. I call on the element of air. Move quickly to activate my purpose and manifest my wishes this coming year. So may it be."
8. Place your sigil spell jar on your altar.
9. Pull a Tarot card message for your year ahead.
10. Blow out the candle.

SOLAR RETURN GEMINI

Happy Birthday, Gemini! Birthdays hold potent energy for spellwork. It's time to honour the return of the sun to the natal chart position that you were born in. Cast this spell to bring new connections for the year ahead.

You will need:

★ A candle
★ A pen and paper
★ A jar
★ Dill
★ A feather
★ A crystal: moonstone
★ Incense
★ Tarot cards

THE SPELL

1. Light the candle.
2. Close your eyes and connect to your intention.
3. Write your birthday wish on a piece of paper.
4. Fold the paper and mark it with the symbols of the sun, Gemini and Mercury.
5. Prepare your spell jar by adding the sigil, herb, feather, crystal and smoke from the incense. Put a lid on the jar to trap the smoke.
6. Hold the jar in your hands and close your eyes.
7. Recite:

   "I honour the sun and my life on this day of my solar return. I call on the element of air. Move quickly to activate my purpose and manifest my wishes this coming year. So may it be."

8. Place your sigil spell jar on your altar.
9. Pull a Tarot card message for your year ahead.
10. Blow out the candle.

SPRING EQUINOX

On the spring equinox, day and night are equally balanced. It usually falls between 20 and 23 March in the Northern Hemisphere, and between 22 and 23 September in the Southern Hemisphere. From here on, the days grow longer. This is the perfect time for planting seeds of intention.

You will need:

★ A candle
★ A packet of seeds
★ A marker
★ A leaf
★ String
★ Access to the outdoors and trees

THE SPELL

1. Light the candle.
2. Place the seeds in your hands.
3. Close your eyes and envision your intention as a seed carried off by the wind to find a place to earth.
4. Write your intention on the leaf.
5. Fold the leaf and mark it with the symbol for earth.
6. Bind it with string.
7. Recite:
   "I call on the element of air to carry this seed and manifest my intention. So may it be."
8. Go outdoors and throw the seeds to the wind.
9. Tie your intention leaf to a tree and let it blow in the wind.
10. Blow out the candle.

BELTANE

Welcome to spring! Beltane is a Pagan celebration of new life and fertility. In the Northern Hemisphere it falls on 1 May. Beltane is a great time to manifest joy, health and vitality.

You will need:

- ★ Flower hair wreath
- ★ A candle
- ★ A charcoal disc
- ★ A cauldron
- ★ A crystal:
  rose quartz or
  aventurine
- ★ A pen and paper
- ★ A Tarot card:
  the Empress
- ★ Herbs: hawthorn,
  mugwort, violet,
  birch, mint,
  daisy, rosemary,
  thyme, yarrow

THE SPELL

1. Put on a flower hair wreath or other clothes associated with Beltane.
2. Light the candle.
3. Light the charcoal disc and place in your cauldron.
4. Place your crystal in your palm or rest it on your body.
5. Focus your awareness on your energy.
6. Recite:
   "I call on the element of air. Descend upon me and move quickly to manifest my intentions."
7. Write down what you want to manifest into your life on a piece of paper.
8. Fold the paper and place it on your altar, with the Empress card on top.
9. Sprinkle some of your Beltane herbal blend on the hot coal.
10. Recite:
    "By the power of air I manifest these things into my life. So may it be."
11. Blow out the candle.

⊛ MY EX WILL TEXT ME

Needing to hear from your ex? Try this simple spell.

△

You will need:

★ Your phone

THE SPELL

1. Find an image of your ex.
2. Close your eyes and focus your awareness on your ex.
3. Envision your ex messaging you.
4. Recite:

   "I call on the element of air to bring communication from my ex. So may it be."
5. Send the photo of your ex to yourself with the word: "Communication".

COMMUNICATION UNBLOCKER

Sometimes communication doesn't flow. Perhaps you've been waiting to hear back from someone via email or text, or there are constant tech mishaps. Here is a spell to unblock the channels!

△

You will need:

★ A candle
★ Tape
★ A feather
★ Your phone, tablet or laptop
★ Rosemary
★ A fan

THE SPELL

1. Light the candle.
2. Tape the feather to your tech device.
3. Light the rosemary and smoke cleanse your device.
4. Fan air over your device as you smoke cleanse.

5. Recite:

   "I call on the element of air to unblock communications. Let them come swiftly to me. So may it be."

6. Blow out the candle.

  # ☼E☼ SPEAK TO THE WIND

Cast this spell on a blustery day, when you need clarity.

You will need:

★ A windy or breezy day

★ A feather

THE SPELL

1. Hold the feather.
2. Focus your awareness on the present moment.
3. Close your eyes and connect with your intention.
4. Feel the breeze moving over you.
5. Honour the sensation of the wind with love.
6. Recite:

   "I call on the element of air and welcome you, wind. Bring clarity around [name the issue]. So may it be."

MANIFEST A HOLIDAY

Manifest your dream vacation with this fun spell.

You will need:

★ A candle
★ A Tarot card: the Eight of Wands
★ A bell
★ Your phone

THE SPELL

1. Light the candle.
2. Place the Eight of Wands card and the bell in front of you.
3. Search for an image of where you want to go on holiday on your phone.
4. Close your eyes and focus your awareness on the good vibes of that holiday.
5. Feel the warmth and positivity of actually being there.
6. Recite:
   "I call on the element of air to blow in the winds of change and manifest my holiday. So may it be."
7. Ring the bell over the image and the Eight of Wands card.
8. Send yourself the image with the words: "So may it be".
9. Blow out the candle.

SCHOOL EXAM SUCCESS

Is exam stress getting you down? Here is a spell to aid your revision and invite success.

You will need:

- ★ A candle
- ★ A Tarot card: the Page of Swords
- ★ A bell
- ★ Your coursework
- ★ Incense
- ★ Your phone

THE SPELL

1. Light the candle.
2. Place the Page of Swords card, the bell and your coursework in front of you.
3. Close your eyes and envision the winds of knowledge blowing in.
4. Recite:

   "I call on the element of air to blow in the winds of knowledge and bring me success in my exams. So may it be."

5. Light the incense and pass the smoke over your coursework.
6. Ring the bell over your coursework.
7. Take a photo and send it to yourself with the word: "Success".
8. Blow out the candle.

SAFE TRAVELS

Here is a spell to help keep you safe as you travel.

You will need:
★ Your phone

THE SPELL

1. Search for the symbol for air on your phone.
2. Close your eyes and focus your awareness on the protective element of air circling you and your vehicle of travel.
3. Recite:

   "I call on the element of air to activate protection and safe travels. So may it be."
4. Send yourself the symbol for air along with the words: "So it may be".

WRITER'S BLOCK CURE

Sometimes words don't flow. Use this spell to banish creative block!

You will need:
★ A candle
★ Tape
★ A feather
★ Pen, pencil or laptop
★ A fan
★ Your phone

THE SPELL

1. Light the candle.
2. Tape the feather to your pen, pencil or laptop.
3. Close your eyes and envision your block and the wind of release blowing away your block.
4. Recite:

   "I call on the element of air to blow in the winds of release to banish my writer's block. So may it be."

5. Fan air over your pen, pencil or laptop with the feather taped to it.

6. Take a photo of the pen, pencil or laptop and send it to yourself with the words: "Writer's block, be gone".

7. Blow out the candle.

 # RECEIVE DOWNLOADS

A download is a spiritual insight that comes to you in a state of awakened consciousness. Receiving these insights can be life-changing and redirect the course of your life path and purpose. Cast this spell to invite downloads.

You will need:

★ A candle

★ A graphic design app like Canva

★ Your phone or laptop

THE SPELL

1. Light the candle.

2. Open the design app on your phone or laptop and create a new design with the words: "I receive downloads".

3. Close your eyes and envision the element of air opening your mind to receive downloads.

4. Recite:
   "I call on the element of air to activate me to receive downloads. So may it be."

5. Download your image and send it to yourself with the words: "So may it be".

6. Blow out the candle.

SEND A TELEPATHIC MESSAGE

This is a fun spell to try with a friend! Let your friend know that you will send them a telepathic message, engage in this spell and then check in with them to see if they received it. (Before engaging in this spell see page 365 for Telepathy Initiation)

You will need:

- ★ A candle
- ★ Your phone
- ★ A crystal: clear quartz
- ★ A fan

THE SPELL

1. Light the candle.
2. Find a photo of the person to whom you intend to send a telepathic message on your phone.
3. Place your phone in front of you with the person's photo on it.
4. Hold the crystal in your hand.
5. Relax into your mediation and envision yourself and the crystal being filled with the powerful energy of communication.
6. Envision the wind blowing your communication to this person.
7. Recite:
   "Through the power of the element of air I send the following message to [name the person]: [speak your message]. So may it be."
8. Use your fan to move air over the image of the person.
9. Blow out the candle.

MERCURY RETROGRADE

Mercury retrograde is thought to spur tech mishaps, miscommunication and travel chaos. Prepare this spell jar to keep you calm and protected during the planet's transit.

You will need:

- ★ A candle
- ★ A pen and paper
- ★ A ribbon
- ★ A jar
- ★ A feather
- ★ Herbs: cinnamon, dill, lavender, liquorice, star anise, thyme
- ★ Incense

THE SPELL

1. Light the candle.
2. Prepare your sigil: you will be using the word: "Protect". Drop the vowels and any duplicate letters so you end up with: "P R T C". Re-write these letters on your piece of paper, arranging them in a creative way, and add the symbol for Mercury.
3. Fold your paper and bind it with the ribbon.
4. Place the sigil, feather, herbs and smoke from the incense in the spell jar. Put a lid on the jar to trap the smoke.
5. On the lid of the jar, draw the symbol for air.
6. Hold the jar in your hands and close your eyes.
7. Recite:
   "I call on the element of air to protect me and all my communications, tech devices and travel during Mercury retrograde. So may it be."
8. Place your sigil spell jar on your altar or near your computer. Leave it there for the duration of the retrograde.
9. Blow out the candle.

BRING SWIFT CHANGE

Sometimes life can feel stale and stagnant. We are ready for a change and a new chapter but don't quite know how to bring it on. This simple and quick spell will get the ball rolling!

You will need:

- ★ A candle
- ★ A feather
- ★ A crystal: clear quartz
- ★ A window

THE SPELL

1. Light the candle.
2. Close your eyes and envision the change you want.
3. Recite:
   "I call on the element of air to blow in the winds of change and connect me to a new chapter in life. So may it be."
4. Place the feather on your windowsill.
5. Put the crystal on top of the feather.
6. Open the window.
7. Recite:
   "I welcome the windows of change. So may it be."
8. Blow out the candle.

HOUSE CLEARING

Have you ever moved into a new home where the energy didn't feel quite right? Here is a housewarming spell to shift out the old energy and welcome the new.

You will need:

- ★ A candle
- ★ A feather
- ★ Rosemary
- ★ A fan
- ★ A crystal: black obsidian
- ★ A window

THE SPELL

1. Light the candle.
2. Close your eyes and envision blowing out your negative energy.
3. Hold the feather and recite:
   "I call on the element of air to blow away the negative energy in this place and replace it with positive energy. So may it be."
4. Light the rosemary and walk around your home, smoke cleansing room-to-room.
5. Fan the smoke through the air.
6. Place the feather on your windowsill.
7. Put the crystal on top of the feather.
8. Open the window.
9. Blow out the candle.

INVITE SYNCHRONICITIES

Sometimes we feel disconnected from the Universe and its messages. Here is a spell to get things flowing again!

You will need:

★ Your phone

THE SPELL

1. Close your eyes and envision the number 11:11.
2. Recite:
   "I call on the element of air to activate synchronicity in my life. So may it be."
3. Type out a message or email with the number 11:11 before blowing air on the screen of your phone.
4. Send the message/email to yourself.
5. Blow air on the screen of your phone again.

PUBLIC SPEAKING

This spell is intended to boost your confidence ahead of a speech or presentation.

You will need:

★ Fennel seeds

THE SPELL

1. Focus your awareness on the present moment and close your eyes.
2. Recite:
   "I call on the element of air to support me with my speech. So may it be."

3. Put some fennel seeds in your mouth and chew.

4. After a few minutes, spit them out.

 # CLEAR NEGATIVE THOUGHTS

Feeling negative? Here is a spell to blow those thoughts away.

You will need:

★ To be outdoors

THE SPELL

1. Focus your awareness on the present moment.

2. Close your eyes and feel the gentle breeze or wind on your skin.

3. Envision the air blowing your thoughts far away.

4. Recite:

   "I call on the element of air to move swiftly to blow these negative thoughts far away. So may it be."

ENACT JUSTICE

There are times when we feel wronged and treated unfairly. This spell will ensure justice prevails.

You will need:

- ★ A candle
- ★ A Tarot card: Justice
- ★ A knife
- ★ A bell
- ★ A crystal: Clear Quartz
- ★ A window

THE SPELL

1. Light the candle.
2. Place the Justice card in front of you, with the knife on top.
3. Close your eyes and focus your awareness on the power of the Justice card and where you want justice in your life.
4. Envision the wind bringing justice.
5. Recite:

   "I call on the element of air to bring me justice. So may it be."

6. Ring the bell over the Justice card, knife and crystal.
7. Open the window and let the breeze enter.
8. Blow out the candle.

CONNECT WITH FAIRIES

Fairies are associated with the earth, but also with the air given they often have wings. At once powerful and playful, fairies bring to mind the trickster archetype, something to be mindful of before working with them. That said, fairies also bring joy, humour and healing, and can help you find missing objects or rid pests from your home.

You will need:

★ A candle
★ A fairy offering (i.e. flowers, trinkets, candy)
★ Crystals: agate, quartz
★ Your phone
★ A bell
★ A pen
★ Your journal or grimoire

THE SPELL

1. Light the candle.
2. Prepare your fairy offering. Place the crystals alongside your choice of items.
3. Search for an image of a fairy on your phone.
4. Close your eyes and focus your awareness on the image.
5. Feel the warmth and positivity of connecting to your fairy guide.
6. Envision the fairy flying toward your offering and crystals.
7. Recite:
   "I call on the element of air to bring connection with my fairy guide. So may it be."
8. Ring the bell to call the fairy in.
9. Sit in meditation.
10. Write down your impressions or insights in your journal or grimoire.
11. Send yourself the image of the fairy with the words: "My guide".
12. Blow out the candle.

RAIN, RAIN, GO AWAY

This weather spell will dispel the rain. Send the clouds where they are more needed. Caution: doing weather spells in your area will have a knock-on effect in other areas.

You will need:

★ Intention

THE SPELL

1. Close your eyes and focus your awareness on the present moment.
2. Recite:
   "I call on the element of air to move swiftly to dispel the clouds and bring sunshine to this area. So may it be."

SUCCESS WITH A MUSIC CAREER

Are you a musician trying to make it? Try this spell to invite success.

You will need:

★ A candle
★ Your phone
★ A bell

THE SPELL

1. Light the candle.
2. Have your phone and a file with your music inside it in front of you.
3. Close your eyes and envision the air element carrying your music to the right contacts, and opportunities flying in.
4. Recite:
   "I call on the element of air to activate success in my music career. So may it be."

5. Ring the bell over your phone.
6. Send yourself the music file with the word: "Success".
7. Blow out the candle.

 # BOOST COGNITION

Experiencing brain fog? Try this simple charm-bag spell to clear your mind.

You will need:

★ A candle
★ Crystals: fluorite, lapis, pyrite citrine, sodalite
★ Herbs: ginkgo and lemon balm
★ Small pouch
★ A bell

THE SPELL

1. Light the candle.
2. Prepare your charm bag by adding the crystals and herbs to a small pouch.
3. Close the pouch and hold it in your hands.
4. Close your eyes and envision thinking lucidly.
5. Recite:
   "I call on the element of air to clear brain fog. So may it be."
6. Ring the bell over your charm bag.
7. Place your charm bag under your pillow.
8. Blow out the candle.

UNLEASH MUSICAL POTENTIAL

Do you feel like you have unutilized musical potential? Unleash it with this crystal spell.

You will need:

★ A candle
★ A musical instrument (if you have one)
★ Crystals: clear quartz, amethyst, blue lace agate, citrine, malachite, carnelian, pyrite, tangerine quartz, aquamarine
★ A bell

THE SPELL

1. Light the candle.
2. Place the instrument (or yourself, if your instrument is your voice) in front of the candle.
3. Hold your chosen crystal in your hand, or create a crystal grid if using more than one.
4. Relax into your mediation and feel the energy moving through you.
5. Envision yourself and the crystal(s) being filled with musical melodies.
6. Move your crystal(s) in a circular motion in the air around your instrument (or your throat).
7. Envision the energy transmitting musical melodies into you.
8. Recite:
   "Through the power of the element of air I activate music within me and I unleash it. So may it be."
9. Ring the bell over your musical instrument (or throat).
10. Blow out the candle.

ROAD TRIP ADVENTURE

Time to hit the road! Cast this spell to invite exploration and adventure.

You will need:

★ A candle
★ Your phone
★ A bell

THE SPELL

1. Light the candle.
2. Search for an image of your ideal road trip on your phone.
3. Close your eyes and focus your awareness on the feelings of excitement and adventure.
4. Envision the element of air blowing in and bringing it to you.
5. Recite:
   "I call on the element of air to manifest my road trip. So may it be."
6. Ring the bell over your phone.
7. Send yourself the image with the words: "So may it be".
8. Blow out the candle.

BANISH THE FEAR OF FLYING

Before your next flight, prepare a charm bag to alleviate your fear of flying. Taking this charm bag through customs could prove interesting, so consider it an opportunity to spread a bit of magic!

You will need:

* ★ Salt
* ★ Herbs: rosemary and lavender
* ★ A crystal: black tourmaline
* ★ A small pouch
* ★ A bell

THE SPELL

1. Place the salt, herbs and crystal in the pouch. Close it.
2. Holding the pouch, close your eyes and envision air blowing in and banishing your fear, replacing it with feelings of peace and calm.
3. Recite:
   "I call on the element of air to banish my fear of flying. So may it be."
4. Ring the bell over your charm bag before placing it in your handbag to carry on the plane.

 # EMOJI MAGIC

This fun tech spell should help turn your mood around!

You will need:

* ★ Your phone

THE SPELL

1. Reflect on your mood.
2. Set an intention to uplift your mood.
3. Choose some positive emojis based on the new mood that you wish to have.

4. Recite:

    "I call on the element of air to blow in the winds of change and shift up my mood. So may it be."

5. Send yourself the chosen emojis with the words: "New mood".

TAROT SPELL FOR INDEPENDENCE

Feeling co-dependent or in need of more personal freedom? This Tarot spell should help you reclaim sovereignty.

You will need:

★ A candle
★ A Tarot card: the Queen of Swords
★ Your phone

THE SPELL

1. Light the candle.
2. Take a photo of the Queen of Swords card on your phone.
3. Close your eyes and focus your awareness on the power of the card.
4. Envision yourself as the Queen of Swords, full of independence and empowerment.
5. Recite:

    "I call on the element of air to activate my independence. So may it be."

6. Send yourself the image of the card with the words: "I am independent".
7. Blow out the candle.

ACTIVATE THE GIFT OF WRITING

This spell will aid you in penning that bestseller or typing that email.

You will need:

★ A candle
★ A pen and paper
★ A jar
★ A crystal:
   clear quartz
★ A feather
★ A bell

THE SPELL

1. Light the candle.
2. Prepare your sigil by drawing your initials in a unique way on a piece of paper, followed by the symbol for air.
3. Fold your paper.
4. Prepare your spell jar by adding the sigil, crystal and feather.
5. Put a lid on the jar.
6. Close your eyes and envision the air energy activating you and your jar.
7. Recite:
   "I call on the element of air to activate the gift of writing. So may it be."
8. Ring the bell over the jar.
9. Place the jar on your altar or near to where you write.
10. Blow out the candle.

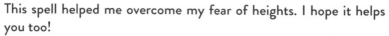

BANISH THE FEAR OF HEIGHTS

This spell helped me overcome my fear of heights. I hope it helps you too!

You will need:

★ A candle
★ Your phone
★ A bell

THE SPELL

1. Light the candle.
2. Search for a photo or video of a person sitting or standing at a great height on your phone.
3. Put your phone with the photo/video in front of you.
4. Close your eyes and imagine you are that person in the image. Notice any feelings.
5. Envision the element of air blowing in to surround and protect you.
6. Recite:
   "I call on the element of air to banish my fear of heights. So may it be."
7. Ring the bell over your phone.
8. Send yourself the video or image with the words: "I banish fear".
9. Blow out the candle.

COLLEGE ACCEPTANCE

Cast this spell to encourage the college of your choice to accept you.

You will need:
- ★ Your phone
- ★ A bell

THE SPELL

1. Take a photo of your filled-out college application form on your phone and place this image in front of you.
2. Close your eyes and feel the energy of change moving through you.
3. Envision your application flying into the right hands and it being accepted.
4. Feel the positive emotions.
5. Recite:

   "I call on the element of air to manifest an acceptance into college. So may it be."
6. Ring the bell over your phone.
7. Send yourself the photo with the word: "Accepted".

RELEASE OBSESSIVE THINKING

Alleviate your obsessive thoughts and restore inner peace with this crystal spell.

You will need:

★ A candle

★ Lavender oil

★ A crystal: red jasper, red goldstone, garnet, amethyst, lepidolite, ametrine

★ A bell

THE SPELL

1. Light the candle.
2. Anoint your third eye and temples with the lavender oil.
3. Hold the crystal in your hand (if using more than one crystal, make a grid).
4. Relax into your mediation and focus your awareness on the element of air.
5. Envision yourself and the crystal being filled with powerful light.
6. Move your crystal(s) in a circular motion around your head.
7. Recite:

   "Through the power of the element of air, banish this obsessive thinking from my mind. Bring peace. So may it be."
8. Ring the bell all around your head.
9. Blow out the candle.

LIE BUSTER

This spell is intended to dismantle lies and show everyone the truth.

You will need:

- ★ A candle
- ★ A Tarot card: the Seven of Swords
- ★ Rosemary
- ★ A fan or feather
- ★ A bell
- ★ Your phone

THE SPELL

1. Light the candle.
2. Place the Seven of Swords card in front of you.
3. Light the rosemary and move the smoke over the card with a fan or feather.
4. Close your eyes and focus your awareness on the power of the card.
5. Recite:
   "I call on the element of air to bust the lies. So may it be."
6. Ring the bell over the card.
7. Send yourself an image of the card with the words: "The truth will be revealed".
8. Blow out the candle.

GOSSIP BINDING

Cast this spell to reduce gossip and lessen its impact.

You will need:

★ Your phone

THE SPELL

1. Close your eyes and set an intention to bind the gossip against you.
2. Prepare a digital sigil by typing the initials of the person gossiping, and then placing the tongue and rope emojis between the letters. Your sigil should look something like this: A 👅 🪢 J.
3. Recite:
   "I call on the element of air to bind the gossiping tongue of [name the person]. So may it be."
4. Send yourself the digital sigil.

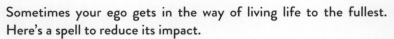

EGO DISSOLUTION

Sometimes your ego gets in the way of living life to the fullest. Here's a spell to reduce its impact.

You will need:

★ A candle
★ Your phone
★ A bell

THE SPELL

1. Light the candle.
2. Close your eyes and focus your awareness on dissolving your ego.
3. Envision not taking yourself too seriously.
4. Feel the joy, positivity and freedom that brings.
5. Take a funny selfie with your phone.
6. Recite:
   "I call on the element of air to dissolve my ego and bring joy. So may it be."
7. Ring the bell over your phone.
8. Post the selfie to social media with the clown emoji.
9. Blow out the candle.

A TAROT SPELL FOR DECISION-MAKING

Feeling indecisive? Here's a Tarot spell to get things moving again.

You will need:

★ A candle
★ Tarot cards
★ A bell

THE SPELL

1. Light the candle.
2. Place the Two of Swords in front of you.
3. Close your eyes and meditate on the choice that you need to make.
4. Envision yourself as the maiden on the Two of Swords card, opening your arms and heart, and removing the blindfold so you can view the sea and the crescent moon.
5. Intuit which decision resonates with your heart.
6. Recite:

   "I call on the element of air to show me the right decision. So may it be."
7. Ring the bell over the Two of Swords card.
8. Take a deep breath and pull a Tarot card for each decision on your mind. Does this reading resonate with what your heart just revealed to you?

✦ FIND A FEATHER

The next time you find a feather, cast this spell to make a wish.

You will need:

★ A found feather
★ Your phone

THE SPELL

1. Hold the feather in your hand.
2. Close your eyes and set an intention toward whatever you wish to manifest.
3. Envision yourself and the feather being filled with the power of movement.
4. Recite:
   "Through the power of the element of air I manifest [name your wish] into my life. So may it be."
5. Send yourself a photo of the feather with the words: "So may it be".

BANISH AN INTERNET TROLL

Protect yourself from bothersome online trolls with this handy banishing spell.

You will need:

★ Your phone

THE SPELL

1. Close your eyes.
2. Set an intention to banish the troll.
3. Prepare a digital sigil combining the handle of the person trolling you with the wind face and devil emojis. Your sigil should

look something like this: la_ 🙂 state.

4. Recite:

   "I call on the element of air to banish the trolling of [name the person]. So may it be."

5. Send yourself the digital sigil.

COMPUTER VIRUS PROTECTION

Here is a spell to help protect your computer from viruses.

You will need:

★ A candle
★ A computer
★ An electric fan
★ Rosemary

THE SPELL

1. Light the candle.
2. Place your computer in front of you, with the electric fan next to it.
3. Close your eyes and set an intention to banish computer viruses.
4. Light the rosemary and smoke-cleanse your computer.
5. Recite:

   "I call on the element of air to keep computer viruses away. So may it be."

6. Turn on the fan and blow air on your computer for 10 minutes.
7. Blow out the candle.

MIND BALANCE

Need to clear your head of racing thoughts? Cast this simple spell to help bring your mind energy balance back into equilibrium.

You will need:

★ A candle
★ Binaural beats or isochronic tones
★ Two crystals: tiger's eye, sodalite, amazonite, smoky quartz, hematite, blue sapphire, zoisite, bloodstone, calcite, amethyst, carnelian, moonstone, larimar or jade
★ A bell

THE SPELL

1. Light the candle.
2. Play the music clip of your choice.
3. Lie down and place two crystals of your choice on either side of your head.
4. Relax into your mediation and envision yourself and the crystals being filled with harmonious balance.
5. Recite:
   "Through the power of the element of air I activate balance in my mind. So may it be."
6. Ring the bell all around your head.
7. Blow out the candle.

INCREASE YOUR FOLLOWERS

Here is a spell to boost your following on social media!

You will need:

★ Your phone

THE SPELL

1. Take a screenshot of your social media page and place your phone in front of you.
2. Close your eyes and set an intention to increase your following.
3. Look at the screen grab of your social media page.
4. Create a digital sigil by using people and checkmark emojis: 👤👥✔.
5. Recite:

   "I call on the element of air to increase my followers on [name social media platform]. So may it be."

6. Send yourself the photo along with the digital sigil.

PROTECT YOUR SOCIAL MEDIA ACCOUNT

The possibility of digital attack from hackers is scary. This protection spell will boost your social media account's security.

You will need:

★ A candle
★ Your phone
★ Rosemary
★ A fan or feather

THE SPELL

1. Light the candle.
2. Take a screenshot of your social media page and then place your phone in front of you.
3. Close your eyes and set an intention to bring in protection.
4. Light the rosemary and move the smoke over your phone with a fan or feather.
5. Recite:
   "I call on the element of air to protect my [name your social media account]. So may it be."
6. Send yourself the image of your social media page and the symbol for protection (see page 8).
7. Blow out the candle.

BANISH AN ONLINE IMPERSONATOR

Unfortunately, online impersonation is common, particularly for business owners and public figures. Here is a spell to discourage impersonators.

You will need:

★ A candle
★ Your phone
★ A crystal: black obsidian

THE SPELL

1. Light the candle.
2. Take a screenshot of the imposter page and then place your phone in front of you.
3. Hold the crystal in your hand.
4. Close your eyes and set an intention to banish the imposter.
5. Move the crystal in a circular motion around your phone.
6. Recite:

   "I call on the element of air to banish the imposter called [name the fake handle]. So may it be."

7. Create a digital sigil with the handle of the imposter and the wind face and silhouette emojis. Your sigil should look something like this: la_ 🌬 well👤 ness_.
8. Send yourself the image of the fake page and this digital sigil.
9. Blow out the candle.

PHONE PROTECTION

Here is a spell to protect your phone from theft or breakage.

You will need:

★ A candle
★ Your phone
★ Rosemary
★ A fan or feather

THE SPELL

1. Light the candle.
2. Search for one of the following protection symbols on your phone: Pentacle, Hamsa, Ankh, Triquetra, Labyrinth, Fairy Star, Dragon, Horned Hand, Om, Athame, Lotus or Turtle.
3. Save one of the protection symbols as your homescreen image.
4. Close your eyes and set an intention to bring in protection.
5. Light the rosemary and move the smoke over your phone with a fan or feather.
6. Recite:
   "I call on the element of air to protect my phone. So may it be."
7. Send yourself a digital sigil with the protection symbol.
8. Blow out the candle.

COMPUTER PROTECTION

Computers are expensive and it's inconvenient when they go wrong on us. Here is a spell to protect your computer from breakage or theft.

You will need:

★ Your phone
★ A candle
★ A bell

THE SPELL

1. Light the candle.
2. Search for one of the following protection symbols on your phone: Pentacle, Hamsa, Ankh, Triquetra, Labyrinth, Fairy Star, Dragon, Horned Hand, Om, Athame, Lotus or Turtle.
3. Save one of the protection symbols as your homescreen image.
4. Close your eyes and set an intention to bring in protection.
5. Recite:
   "I call on the element of air to protect my computer. So may it be."
6. Ring the bell around your computer.
7. On your computer, begin an email to yourself. Make the subject field "Protection". In the body of your email, add a digital sigil with the protection symbol. Send this email to yourself.
8. Blow out the candle.

BANISH IMPOSTER SYNDROME

Have you ever been successful at something and then felt like a fraud when presented with a trophy? This is imposter syndrome, and it can become an obstacle if it disrupts your life or prevents you from pursuing your dreams. Here is a spell to help banish it.

You will need:
- ★ A candle
- ★ A pen and paper
- ★ A ribbon
- ★ A bell

THE SPELL

1. Light the candle.
2. Prepare your sigil: you will be using the words "Imposter syndrome". Drop the vowels and any duplicate letters so you end up with: "M P S T R Y N D". Re-write these letters on your piece of paper, arranging them in a creative way, and add the symbol for air.
3. Hold your sigil.
4. Close your eyes and feel the energy of air blowing away any self-doubt.
5. Envision yourself and the sigil filled with powerful energy.
6. Recite:
   "I call on the element of air to banish my imposter syndrome. So may it be."
7. Roll your paper sigil up and tie the ribbon around it.
8. Ring the bell over your sigil.
9. Place your sigil on your altar.

BANISH A NOSY NEIGHBOUR

Nosy neighbours? Cast this spell to keep them on the other side of the fence!

You will need:

* A candle
* A small pouch
* Some salt
* Rosemary
* A feather
* A crystal: black tourmaline
* A ribbon

THE SPELL

1. Light the candle.
2. Prepare your spell pouch by adding the salt, herb, feather and crystal.
3. Close your eyes and envision the air creating a protective shield around your door.
4. Envision the energy moving into your spell pouch.
5. Recite:
   "I call on the element of air to banish my neighbour from my property. So may it be."
6. Tie the ribbon to your pouch.
7. Hang your pouch at your gate, fence or front door. Leave it there for as long as you need.
8. Blow out the candle.

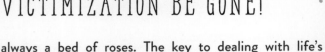

VICTIMIZATION BE GONE!

Life isn't always a bed of roses. The key to dealing with life's challenges is to make sure we take care of ourselves. During times where we put our needs aside, we can end up feeling like a martyr. We put other people's needs before our own, and this may result in feelings of victimization. Here is a spell to help you seek freedom.

You will need:

★ A candle
★ A Tarot card: the Eight of Swords
★ A bell
★ Your phone

THE SPELL

1. Light the candle.
2. Place the Eight of Swords card in front of you.
3. Close your eyes and focus your awareness on the power of the Eight of Swords.
4. Envision yourself as the maiden, bound and blindfolded, with the bounds breaking and blindfold coming free.
5. Set an intention to set yourself free.
6. Recite:

   "I call on the element of air to banish victimization and activate my freedom. So may it be."

7. Ring the bell over the Tarot card.
8. Send yourself an image of the card with the words: "I am free".
9. Blow out the candle.

⟨E⟩ WIND CHIME

The melodic sound of a wind chime is a lullaby sung by the element of air. This song can lift the mood, soothe, create an ethereal atmosphere and manifest your wishes. Cast this wish spell when you next come across a wind chime.

△

You will need:

★ A wind chime
★ Your phone

THE SPELL

1. Stand underneath the wind chime and close your eyes.

2. Think about whatever it is you wish to manifest.

3. Envision yourself and the wind chime being filled with the power of movement.

4. Recite:

   "Through the power of the element of air I manifest [name your wish] into my life. So may it be."

5. Send yourself a photo of the wind chime with the words: "So may it be".

BRAINSTORM INSPIRATION

You are about to have a work meeting and you have the worst brain fog ever. You need to sharpen up your mind for a brainstorming session. Try this spell on the go to fire up your neurons.

You will need:

★ Your phone

THE SPELL

1. Close your eyes and set an intention to activate your brainstorm potential.
2. Picture blowing away the cobwebs from your mind.
3. Recite:
   "I call on the element of air to activate my brainstorm mind. So may it be."
4. Send yourself a digital sigil with your initials and the wind face and cobweb emojis. Your sigil should look something like this: T🌬️🕸️C.

NINE OF SWORDS TAROT

We've all experienced Nine of Swords moments in our lives – they can involve overthinking, anxiety and worries. Here is a spell to help face these challenges, overcome obsessive thoughts and restore balance.

You will need:

★ A candle
★ A Tarot card: the Nine of Swords
★ Rosemary
★ A fan or feather

THE SPELL

1. Light the candle.
2. Place the Nine of Swords card in front of you.
3. Close your eyes and set an intention to dissolve the challenges you are currently up against.
4. Envision yourself as the character on the card. Witness as the scene transforms into something more positive.
5. Light the rosemary and move the smoke over the card with a fan or feather.
6. Recite:
   "I call on the element of air to dissolve [name the issue] and restore balance. So may it be."
7. Blow out the candle.

STOP MAKING ASSUMPTIONS

Making assumptions can negatively impact our relationships with others and impede communication. If you have the tendency to make assumptions in your relationships, use this numerology spell.

You will need:

★ A pen and paper
★ A candle
★ A ribbon
★ A bell

THE SPELL

1. Prepare by finding your number. Write down your full name and the word: "Assumption", and count the number of letters in your group of words. Then add these numbers together (so if you have 19 letters, 1+9=10). If this number is a double digit, add them together again so you end with a single number.

2. Light the candle.

3. Draw your number on a piece of paper.

4. Close your eyes and envision your number and the air blowing it away.

5. Recite:

   "I call on the element of air to banish my tendency to make assumptions. So may it be."

6. Roll your numbered paper up, tie the ribbon around it and put it on your altar.

7. Ring the bell over the paper the same amount of times as your number.

8. Blow out the candle.

PROTECT YOUR EMAIL
FROM HACKERS

Social media platforms are always subject to digital attack. The threat of hackers can leave us feeling vulnerable, particularly when our emails hold valuable information and contacts. Try this protection spell to help secure your account and repel hackers.

You will need:

★ A candle
★ Your computer or phone
★ A bell

THE SPELL

1. Light the candle.
2. Place your computer or phone in front of you.
3. Close your eyes and set an intention to bring in protection.
4. Recite:
   "I call on the element of air to protect my email account. So may it be."
5. Ring the bell around your computer or phone.
6. On your device, start writing an email to yourself with the subject field as "Protection". In the body of your email, type out the digital sigil of protection (see page 8). Email this to yourself.
7. Blow out the candle.

STOP VISITING YOUR
EX'S SOCIAL MEDIA

After a breakup, it's often challenging to avoid peeping at your ex's social media account. But succumbing to this temptation is seldom rewarding, often bringing up all sorts of unpleasant feelings. This spell will give you the strength to move on.

You will need:

★ A candle
★ Your phone
★ Rosemary
★ A fan or feather

THE SPELL

1. Light the candle.
2. Take a screenshot of your ex's social media page and keep it open in front of you.
3. Close your eyes and set an intention to bring in strength to stop visiting this page.
4. Light the rosemary and move the smoke over your phone with a fan or feather.
5. Recite:

   "I call on the element of air to stop me from visiting [name your ex]'s social media page. So may it be."

6. Send yourself the image of your ex's page and a digital sigil with lion and phone emojis, like this: 🦁📱🦁.
7. Blow out the candle.

IMPECCABLE WORDS

Words are a potent form of magic. You can uplift a person through words or you can devastate them. If you tend to hurt people through the things you say, this spell may be for you!

You will need:

★ A candle
★ A pen and paper
★ A feather
★ A crystal: rose quartz

THE SPELL

1. Light the candle.
2. Prepare your sigil: you will be using the words "I speak words of love". Drop the vowels and any duplicate letters so you end up with: "S P K W R D F L V". Re-write these letters on your piece of paper, arranging them in a creative way, and add the symbol for air.
3. Hold your sigil and crystal.
4. Close your eyes and envision air moving through you.
5. Picture yourself and the sigil filled with powerful love.
6. Recite:

    "I call on the element of air to activate my impeccable words. So may it be."

7. Place the sigil on your altar and put the feather and crystal on top of it.

GOOD VIBES

This spell should help shift the cloud hanging over your head, and bring back good vibes.

You will need:

★ Your phone

THE SPELL

1. Close your eyes and invite good vibes.
2. Recite:

   "I call on the element of air to activate good vibes. So may it be."

3. Send yourself a digital sigil with your initials and the wind face and sparkle emojis. Your sigil should look something like this: T✦C.

SOCIAL BUTTERFLY

You are on your way to a party but you are not feeling up for it. This spell can be cast on the go to invoke your inner social butterfly. You will soon be able to access a wealth of confidence, charisma and charm. Conversations will flow easily.

You will need:

★ Your phone

THE SPELL

1. Close your eyes and set an intention to invoke your inner social butterfly.
2. Recite:

   "I call on the element of air to invoke my inner social butterfly. So may it be."

3. Send yourself a digital sigil with your initials and the wind face and butterfly emojis. Your sigil should look something like this: T 🌬️ 🦋 C.

RECEIVE A PHONE CALL

Waiting around for that promised phone call? Or has it just been a while since colleagues, family or friends have reached out? This spell will encourage others to call and initiate conversations with you.

You will need:

★ Your phone

THE SPELL

1. Close your eyes and set an intention to receive a phone call from a specific person.

2. Recite:
   "I call on the element of air to bring me a phone call from [name the person]. So may it be."

3. Send yourself a digital sigil with your initials and the wind face and phone emojis. Your sigil should look something like this: T C.

BANISH IMPULSIVENESS

Impulsive behaviour can cause regrets as well as create destructive situations in our personal life, relationships and work life. This numerology spell will help banish impulsiveness and create more balance.

△

You will need:

★ A pen and paper
★ A candle
★ A ribbon
★ A bell

THE SPELL

1. Prepare by finding your number. Write down your full name and the word: "Impulsive", and count the number of letters in your group of words. Then add these numbers together (so if you have 19 letters, 1+9=10). If this number is a double digit, add them together again so you end with a single number.

2. Light the candle.

3. Draw your number on a piece of paper.

4. Close your eyes and envision your number and the air blowing it away.

5. Recite:

   "I call on the element of air to banish my impulsiveness. So may it be."

6. Roll up your numbered paper, tie the ribbon around it and put it on your altar.

7. Ring the bell over the paper the same amount of times as your number.

8. Blow out the candle.

RESTORE HARMONY AFTER ARGUING

An argument can feel like a hurricane. Afterwards, everything feels upside down and unsettled. Here is a numerology spell to help blow away chaos and restore order.

You will need:

★ A pen and paper
★ A candle
★ A ribbon
★ A bell

THE SPELL

1. Prepare by finding your number: write down your full name and the word: "Harmony", and count the number of letters in your group of words. Then add these numbers together (so if you have 19 letters, 1+9=10). If this number is a double digit, add them together again so you end with a single number.
2. Light the candle.
3. Draw your number on a piece of paper.
4. Close your eyes and envision your number and the air blowing it away.
5. Recite:

   "I call on the element of air to restore order after my argument with [name the person]. So may it be."
6. Tie the ribbon around your numbered paper and put it on your altar.
7. Ring the bell over top of the paper the same amount of times as your number.
8. Blow out the candle.

⊜ NEW INVENTION

The element of air provides potent energy for new ideas and innovation. If you are an ideas person and always looking to invent something new, try this spell to manifest a new invention.

You will need:
★ Your phone

THE SPELL

1. Close your eyes and set an intention to receive a new idea.
2. Recite:
   "I call on the element of air to bring me a new idea. So may it be."
3. Send yourself a digital sigil with your initials and the wind face and lightbulb emojis. Your sigil should look something like this: T 🌬️💡C.

⊜ RECEIVE AN EMAIL RESPONSE

Expecting an email response? This spell will help expedite things!

You will need:
★ Your phone

THE SPELL

1. Close your eyes and set an intention to receive an email.
2. Recite:
   "I call on the element of air to bring me an email. So may it be."

AIR SPELLS

3. Send yourself a digital sigil with
your initials and the wind face and
laptop emojis. Your sigil should look
something like this: T 🌬 ▪️C.

✦ ATTRACT KINDNESS

Sometimes we just need kindness. This can be from others or from
within ourselves. Kindness shifts energy and brings more magic into
the world. Here is a spell to make the world kinder.

You will need:

★ Your phone

THE SPELL

1. Close your eyes and set an
intention to be kind.

2. Recite:

*"I call on the element of air to bring
me kindness. So may it be."*

3. Send yourself a digital sigil with your
initials and the wind face and happy
face emojis. Your sigil should look
something like this: T 🌬 😊 C.

⟨E⟩ RECEIVE KNOWLEDGE

Studying or doing research? Cast this spell to help advance your knowledge of a topic.

△

You will need:
★ Your phone

THE SPELL

1. Close your eyes and set an intention to receive knowledge.

2. Recite:
   "I call on the element of air to bring me knowledge. So may it be."

3. Send yourself a digital sigil with the face blowing wind, books and sparkle emojis. Your sigil should look like this: 🌬️ 📚 ✨

MAKE A WISH ON
A BUTTERFLY

Butterflies bring joy and happiness. They are also great symbols of transformation. Next time you see a butterfly, cast this wish spell.

You will need:

★ A butterfly

THE SPELL

1. Spot the butterfly.
2. Close your eyes and envision the element of air moving through you.
3. Connect to the transformative magic of the butterfly.
4. Set an intention.
5. Recite:

   "I call on the element of air to bring me my wish of [name the wish]. So may it be."

FIRE
SPELLS

Work with the elemental magic of fire in summer for all things related to purification, protection, initiation, activation, recharging, renewal, alchemy, transformation, inspiration and big passions. The most common forms of using fire magic involve candles, flames, burning, heating, sex and the sun. In each of the fire spells, is it important to envision the energy of the fire moving through you, contributing its power to your intentions.

NEW MOON IN SAGITTARIUS

The new moon is the perfect time for setting an intention to manifest something new into your life. The new moon in Sagittarius is powerful when calling in energies of passion, independence and assertiveness.

△

You will need:

★ A knife
★ A candle
★ A charcoal disc
★ A cauldron
★ A pen and paper
★ Sage
★ A Tarot card: Temperance

THE SPELL

1. With your knife, carve the symbol for Sagittarius into your candle.
2. Light the candle.
3. Light the charcoal disc and place in your cauldron.
4. Focus on your intention and visualize it coming into being.
5. Write your intention on a piece of paper.
6. Fold the paper and mark it with the symbols for the new moon, Sagittarius and Jupiter.
7. Sprinkle some sage on the hot coal.
8. Close your eyes.
9. Recite:

   "By the power of the new moon in Sagittarius and the element of fire, I manifest my intention. So may it be."

10. Place your sigil on your altar and put the Temperance card on top of it.
11. Blow out the candle.

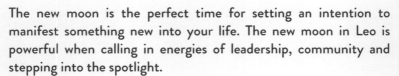

NEW MOON IN LEO

The new moon is the perfect time for setting an intention to manifest something new into your life. The new moon in Leo is powerful when calling in energies of leadership, community and stepping into the spotlight.

△

You will need:

★ A knife
★ A candle
★ A charcoal disc
★ A cauldron
★ A pen and paper
★ Sunflower petals
★ A Tarot card: Strength

THE SPELL

1. With your knife, carve the symbol for Leo into your candle.
2. Light the candle.
3. Light the charcoal disc and place in your cauldron.
4. Focus on your intention and visualize it coming into being.
5. Write your intention on a piece of paper.
6. Fold the paper and mark it with the symbols for the new moon, Leo and the sun.
7. Sprinkle some sunflower petals on the hot coal.
8. Close your eyes.
9. Recite:
   "By the power of the new moon in Leo and the element of fire, I manifest my intention. So may it be."
10. Place your sigil on your altar and put the Strength card on top of it.
11. Blow out the candle.

NEW MOON IN ARIES

The new moon is the perfect time for setting an intention to manifest something new into your life. The new moon in Aries is powerful when calling in energies of confidence, determination and passion.

△

You will need:

★ A knife
★ A candle
★ A charcoal disc
★ A cauldron
★ A pen and paper
★ Wormwood
★ A Tarot card:
   the Emperor

THE SPELL

1. With your knife, carve the symbol for Aries into your candle.
2. Light the candle.
3. Light the charcoal disc and place in your cauldron.
4. Focus on your intention and visualize it coming into being.
5. Write your intention on a piece of paper.
6. Fold the paper and mark it with the symbols for the new moon, Aries and Mars.
7. Sprinkle some wormwood on the hot coal.
8. Close your eyes.
9. Recite:

   "By the power of the new moon in Aries and the element of fire, I manifest my intention. So may it be."

10. Place your sigil on your altar and put the Emperor card on top of it.
11. Blow out the candle.

FULL MOON IN SAGITTARIUS

The full moon is the ideal time for letting go of things that no longer serve you. During this event of great catharsis and wholeness, emotions from the deep unconscious come up to the light to integrate. The full moon in Sagittarius is powerful when releasing energies of restlessness, arguments and hot-headedness.

△

You will need:

★ A candle
★ A charcoal disc
★ A cauldron
★ A pen and paper
★ A crystal: aquamarine
★ Sage

THE SPELL

1. Light the candle.
2. Light the charcoal disc and place in your cauldron.
3. Focus your awareness on your emotional wellbeing. Notice any emotions or thoughts that arise.
4. Write down what you want to release on a piece of paper. Fold the paper.
5. Hold the aquamarine crystal in your hand.
6. Recite:

   "I call on the element of fire. Move quickly to burn away that which no longer serves me."
7. Sprinkle some sage on the hot coal.
8. Light your paper and place it in your cauldron. Allow the paper to burn to ash.
9. Recite:

   "By the power of the full moon in Sagittarius, I set myself free. So may it be."
10. Blow out the candle.

FULL MOON IN LEO

The full moon is the ideal time for letting go of things that no longer serve you. During this event of great catharsis and wholeness, emotions from the deep unconscious come up to the light to integrate. The full moon in Leo is powerful when releasing energies of egotism, possessiveness and vanity.

You will need:

★ A candle
★ A charcoal disc
★ A cauldron
★ A pen and paper
★ A crystal: labradorite
★ A sunflower

THE SPELL

1. Light the candle.
2. Light the charcoal disc and place in your cauldron.
3. Focus your awareness on your emotional wellbeing. Notice any emotions or thoughts that arise.
4. Write down what you want to release on a piece of paper and then fold the paper.
5. Hold the crystal in your hand.
6. Recite:

   "I call on the element of fire. Move quickly to burn away that which no longer serves me."
7. Sprinkle the petals of your sunflower on the hot coal.
8. Light your paper and place it in your cauldron. Allow the paper to burn to ash.
9. Recite:

   "By the power of the full moon in Leo, I set myself free. So may it be."
10. Blow out the candle.

FULL MOON IN ARIES

The full moon is the ideal time for letting go of things that no longer serve you. During this event of great catharsis and wholeness, emotions from the deep unconscious come up to the light to integrate. The full moon in Aries is powerful when releasing energies of aggression, selfishness and recklessness.

△

You will need:

★ A candle
★ A charcoal disc
★ A cauldron
★ A pen and paper
★ A crystal: obsidian
★ Wormwood

THE SPELL

1. Light the candle.
2. Light the charcoal disc and place in your cauldron.
3. Focus your awareness on your emotional wellbeing. Notice any emotions or thoughts that arise.
4. Write down what you want to release on a piece of paper. Fold the paper.
5. Hold the crystal in your hand.
6. Recite:

   "I call on the element of fire. Move quickly to burn away that which no longer serves me."
7. Sprinkle some wormwood on the hot coal.
8. Light your paper and place it in your cauldron. Allow the paper to burn to ash.
9. Recite:

   "By the power of the full moon in Aries, I set myself free. So may it be."
10. Blow out the candle.

SOLAR RETURN SAGITTARIUS

Happy Birthday, Sagittarius! Birthdays hold potent energy for spellwork. It's time to honour the return of the sun to the natal chart position that you were born in. Cast this spell to manifest your full potential this year.

△

You will need:

★ A candle
★ A charcoal disc
★ A cauldron
★ Sage
★ A pen and paper
★ Tarot cards

THE SPELL

1. Light the candle.
2. Light the charcoal disc and place in your cauldron.
3. Close your eyes and connect to your intentions.
4. Write your birthday wish on the paper.
5. Fold the paper and mark it with the symbols for the sun, Sagittarius and Jupiter.
6. Sprinkle some sage on the hot coal.
7. Close your eyes.
8. Recite:

   "I honour the sun and my life on this day of my solar return. I call on the element of fire. Move quickly to activate my purpose and manifest my wishes this coming year. So may it be."

9. Place your birthday wish on your altar.
10. Pull a Tarot card message for your year ahead.
11. Blow out the candle.

SOLAR RETURN LEO

It's your birthday, Leo! Birthdays hold potent energy for spellwork. It's time to honour the return of the sun to the natal chart position that you were born in. Cast this spell to step into the spotlight this year.

△

You will need:

★ A candle
★ A charcoal disc
★ A cauldron
★ A pen and paper
★ A sunflower
★ Tarot cards

THE SPELL

1. Light the candle.
2. Light the charcoal disc and place in your cauldron.
3. Close your eyes and connect to your intention.
4. Write your birthday wish on a piece of paper.
5. Fold the paper and mark it with the symbols for the sun and Leo.
6. Sprinkle some sunflower petals on the hot coal.
7. Close your eyes.
8. Recite:

   "I honour the sun and my life on this day of my solar return. I call on the element of fire. Move quickly to activate my purpose and manifest my wishes this coming year. So may it be."
9. Place your birthday wish on your altar.
10. Pull a Tarot card message for your year ahead.
11. Blow out the candle.

SOLAR RETURN ARIES

Happy Birthday, Aries! Birthdays hold potent energy for spellwork. It's time to honour the return of the sun to the natal chart position that you were born in. Cast this spell to help you take action this year.

△

You will need:

★ A candle
★ A charcoal disc
★ A cauldron
★ A pen and paper
★ Wormwood
★ Tarot cards

THE SPELL

1. Light the candle.
2. Light the charcoal disc and place in your cauldron.
3. Close your eyes and connect to your intention.
4. Write your birthday wish on a piece of paper.
5. Fold the paper and mark it with the symbols for the sun, Aries and Mars.
6. Sprinkle some wormwood on the hot coal.
7. Close your eyes.
8. Recite:

   "I honour the sun and my life on this day of my solar return. I call on the element of fire. Move quickly to activate my purpose and manifest my wishes this coming year. So may it be."

9. Place your birthday wish on your altar.
10. Pull a Tarot card message for your year ahead.
11. Blow out the candle.

LION'S GATE

The Lion's Gate portal opening is an annual alignment between the sun in Leo and the ancient star Sirius. The cosmic energies from this alignment are at their highest vibration on 8 August (8/8). The number "8" is an infinity symbol, and corresponds with the Strength Tarot card. Use this spell when you need psychic strength.

You will need:

★ A knife
★ A candle
★ A charcoal disc
★ A cauldron
★ Crystals: amethyst, selenite, clear quartz, lemurian quartz, citrine, celestite
★ A pen and paper
★ A Tarot card: Strength
★ A sunflower

THE SPELL

1. With your knife, carve 88 into your candle.
2. Light the candle.
3. Light the charcoal disc and place in your cauldron.
4. Place your crystals either in a grid or on the areas of your body that you want to activate.
5. Recite:
   "I call on the element of fire from the south and the cosmic energy of the Lion's Gate portal. Descend upon me and move quickly to manifest my intentions."
6. Write down the manifestation that you wish to bring into your life and the number 88.
7. Fold the paper and place it on your altar, with the Strength card on top.
8. Sprinkle some sunflower petals in the cauldron.
9. Recite:
   "By the power of Lion's Gate portal, the star Sirius and the plant ally of sunflower, I manifest an upgrade in my life. So may it be."
10. Blow out the candle.

SUMMER SOLSTICE

Midsummer occurs annually, on the day with the longest period of light, usually on 20 or 21 June in the Northern Hemisphere. Cast this spell to call forth joy, positivity, health and vitality.

△

You will need:

★ A knife
★ A candle
★ A charcoal disc
★ A cauldron
★ Crystals: red jasper, carnelian, citrine, orange calcite, red tiger's eye, sunstone
★ A pen and paper
★ A Tarot card: the Sun
★ Herbs: St. John's Wort, chamomile, calendula, lavender, fennel, mugwort, hemp, rosemary, thyme, verbena, sage, mint, elder, rose, meadowsweet
★ Pestle and mortar

Preparation:

★ Grind the herbs into a herbal blend.

THE SPELL

1. With your knife, carve the symbol for the sun into your candle.
2. Light the candle.
3. Light the charcoal disc and place in your cauldron.
4. Place your crystals either in a grid or on the areas of your body that you want to activate.
5. Recite:
   "I call on the element of fire and the life-giving energy of the sun. Descend upon me and move quickly to activate joy, positivity and fun in my life and manifest my intentions."
6. Write down the manifestation that you wish to bring into your life.
7. Fold the piece of paper and put it on your altar with the Sun card on top.
8. Sprinkle some of your midsummer herbal blend on the hot coal.
9. Recite:
   "By the power of the sun I manifest these things into my life. So may it be."
10. Blow out the candle.

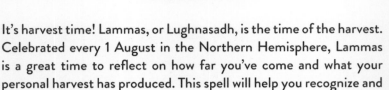

LAMMAS

It's harvest time! Lammas, or Lughnasadh, is the time of the harvest. Celebrated every 1 August in the Northern Hemisphere, Lammas is a great time to reflect on how far you've come and what your personal harvest has produced. This spell will help you recognize and enjoy your abundance.

△

You will need:

- ★ A knife
- ★ A candle
- ★ A charcoal disc
- ★ A cauldron
- ★ Offerings: bread, corn, apples or grain
- ★ A crystal: malachite or sardonyx
- ★ A pen and paper
- ★ A Tarot card: the Empress
- ★ Herbs: meadowsweet, vervain, yarrow, mint, goldenrod
- ★ Pestle and mortar

THE SPELL

1. Using your knife, carve the symbol for fire into your candle.
2. Light the candle.
3. Light the charcoal disc and place in your cauldron.
4. Lay your offerings on your altar.
5. Place the crystal in your palm or rest it on your body.
6. Recite:
   "I call on the element of fire. Descend upon me and move quickly to manifest my intentions."
7. Write down the manifestation that you want to bring into your life.
8. Fold the paper and place it on your altar, with the Empress card on top.
9. Sprinkle some of your herbal blend on the hot coal.
10. Recite:
    "By the power of fire I manifest these things into my life. So may it be."
11. Blow out the candle.

FIRE SPELLS

CONFIDENCE BOOSTER

We all go through times when we have low self-esteem. Always know that it too shall pass. In the meantime, here is a confidence-boosting spell to help things along.

△

You will need:

★ Fresh ginger root
★ A knife
★ A teapot
★ Boiling water
★ A candle
★ A charcoal disc
★ A cauldron
★ A crystal: citrine
★ Tarot cards

THE SPELL

1. First, make your ginger tea by chopping the fresh ginger. Place it in a teapot with boiling water to steep for 10 minutes.
2. With your knife, carve the symbol for fire into your candle.
3. Light the candle.
4. Light the charcoal disc and place in your cauldron.
5. Drink your ginger tea as you focus on the warmth of the ginger moving through you.
6. Hold the crystal in your hand against your solar plexus.
7. Recite:
   "I am here. I am confident. I am connected to my purpose."
8. Invite the elemental magic of fire to activate you by reciting:
   "I call on the power of fire to activate my solar plexus. I am confident. So may it be."
9. Pull a Tarot card for an encouraging message.
10. Blow out the candle.

SEX DRIVE

There are times when our libido wanes. This is totally normal, but sometimes it can get us down. Here is a spell to activate your sacral chakra and recharge your drive!

△

You will need:

★ Maca powder
★ A teapot
★ Boiling water
★ A knife
★ A candle
★ A crystal: red jasper
★ Tarot cards

THE SPELL

1. First, make your maca tea. Put two scoops of the maca powder in a teapot with boiling water, stir thoroughly, and leave to steep for 10 minutes.
2. With your knife, carve the symbol for fire into your candle.
3. Light the candle.
4. Drink your maca tea as you focus on the warmth of the maca moving through you.
5. Hold the crystal in your hand against your belly or genitals.
6. Recite:
   "I am here. I desire. I am sensual. I am free."
7. Invite the elemental magic of fire to activate you by reciting:
   "I call on the power of fire to activate my sacral chakra. I am sexually activated. So may it be."
8. Pull a Tarot card for an encouraging message.
9. Blow out the candle.

SEXY AF

Sometimes you may feel hot and ready for intimate connection, but frustratingly you don't have a partner. Here is a spell to sexually attract a partner.

△

You will need:

- ★ Shatavari root powder
- ★ A teapot
- ★ Boiling water
- ★ A candle
- ★ A crystal: carnelian
- ★ A pen
- ★ A bay leaf
- ★ A Tarot card: the Lovers

THE SPELL

1. First, make your shatavari tea. Add the shatavari root powder to a tea pot with boiling water, stir thoroughly, and leave to steep for 10 minutes.

2. With your knife, carve the symbol for fire into your candle.

3. Light the candle.

4. Drink your shatavari tea as you focus on the warmth of the shatavari moving through you.

5. Hold the crystal in your hand against your belly or genitals.

6. Recite:
   "I am here. I am desirable. I am desired."

7. Write the initials of your desired lover on the bay leaf and place this on your altar. Put the Lovers card on top of the bay leaf.

8. Invite the elemental magic of fire to activate you by reciting:
   "I call on the power of fire to activate my sacral chakra. I am sexually attractive. So may it be."

9. Blow out the candle.

PROVIDE A PICK-ME-UP

Feeling flat and in need of a pick-me-up? This spell is designed to activate your heart chakra and bring more joy into your life.

△

You will need:

★ Lemon balm
★ A teapot
★ A knife
★ A candle
★ A charcoal disc
★ A cauldron
★ A crystal:
   rose quartz
★ Basil
★ Tarot cards

THE SPELL

1. First, make your lemon tea. Add two scoops of lemon balm to a teapot with boiling water and leave it to steep for 10 minutes.
2. With your knife, carve the symbol for fire into your candle.
3. Light the candle.
4. Light the charcoal disc and place in your cauldron.
5. Drink your lemon tea as you focus on the warmth of the lemon balm moving through you.
6. Hold the crystal against your heart chakra.
7. Recite:
   "I am here. I am loved. I love."
8. Sprinkle some basil on the hot coal.
9. Invite the elemental magic of fire to activate you by saying:
   "I call on the power of fire to activate my heart chakra. I am full of joy. So may it be."
10. Pull a Tarot card for an encouraging message.
11. Blow out the candle.

⟨E⟩ ENERGY BOOST

Modern life can be hectic and we are always on the go. This can leave us feeling fatigued. Here is a quick spell to boost your energy!

△

You will need:

★ The sun

THE SPELL

1. Focus your awareness on the sun.
2. Close your eyes and feel the warmth and energy of the sun.
3. Recite:
   "I am here. I am alive. Thank you, sun."
4. Continue to feel the warmth and the brightness on your eyelids.
5. Recite:
   "I call on the power of the sun and the element of fire to boost my energy and my vitality. Charge me up. So may it be."

ATTRACT SUCCESS

You work hard! But sometimes we need a bit of a lucky break. Here is a spell to invite success.

You will need:

★ The sun
★ Your phone

THE SPELL

1. Focus your awareness on the sun.
2. Close your eyes and feel the warmth and energy of the sun.
3. Recite:
   "I am here. I am alive. Thank you, sun."
4. Continue to feel the warmth and the brightness on your eyelids.
5. Focus on the area of your life where you want to bring success.
6. Recite:
   "I call on the power of the sun and the element of fire to bring success into my life. So may it be."
7. Send yourself a photo of the sun with the words: "So may it be".

Ⓔ SUNSET RELEASE

Sometimes we can feel heavy, as if we're holding too much within us. Hell, we can feel like this on a daily basis! For this spell we turn to the daily rhythms of the sun for magical help, to release blocks, find closure and a sense of peace.

△

You will need:

★ The sun

★ Your phone

THE SPELL

1. Focus your awareness on the sun.

2. Close your eyes and feel the warmth and energy of the sun.

3. Recite:
   "I am here. I am alive. Thank you, sun."

4. Continue to feel the warmth and the brightness on your eyelids.

5. Focus on the area of your life where you need release.

6. Recite:
   "I call in the power of the setting sun and the element of fire to release me from [name the issue]. So may it be."

7. Send yourself a photo of the setting sun with the words: "So it may be".

SUNRISE INITIATING

We all sometimes wake up with the feeling we have lost purpose, or confused about our life path. The daily rhythms of the sun can help us magically to reinstil purpose into our lives and feel energized.

You will need:

★ The sun
★ Your phone

THE SPELL

1. Focus your awareness on the sun.
2. Close your eyes and feel the warmth and energy of the sun.
3. Recite:
   "I am here. I am alive. Thank you, sun."
4. Continue to feel the warmth and the brightness on your eyelids.
5. Focus on the area of your life that you need help with.
6. Recite:
   "I call on the power of the rising sun and the element of fire to help me with [name the issue]. So may it be."
7. Send yourself a photo of the rising sun with the words: "So may it be".

DRAGON POWER

Does your spirit feel called to work with dragons? These powerful fire creatures are psychic messengers of balance, and the embodiment of primordial power. They come to us when we need fortitude, courage and strength. Before and after this spell, it is important to ground.

△

You will need:

★ A candle
★ A charcoal disc
★ A cauldron
★ Resin: dragon's blood
★ A crystal: septarian (dragon stone)
★ Tarot cards
★ A pen
★ Your journal or grimoire

THE SPELL

1. Light the candle.
2. Light the charcoal disc and place it in your cauldron.
3. Sprinkle some dragon's blood resin on the hot coal.
4. Focus your awareness on your heart chakra and hold your dragon stone against it.
5. Recite:
   "I am here. I am connected. I am ready."
6. Invite the power of the dragon and the elemental magic of fire to activate by reciting:
   "I call on the power of the dragon to connect with me. Teach me. Transform me. So may it be."
7. Pull a Tarot card for an encouraging message.
8. Write down your experiences in your journal or grimoire.
9. Blow out the candle.

PHOENIX

Are you at a low point in your life? The phoenix is a powerful and mystical bird of rebirth and regeneration, known to die and come back from the ashes. Whether you are navigating endings, loss, grief or heartbreak, cast this spell to rise up from the ashes like the phoenix. Phoenix power is alchemy! Only work with Phoenix if your spirit feels the calling.

△

You will need:

★ A candle
★ A charcoal disc
★ A cauldron
★ Cypress leaves
★ A crystal: phoenix stone
★ Tarot cards
★ A pen
★ Your journal or grimoire

THE SPELL

1. Light the candle.
2. Light the charcoal disc and place it in your cauldron.
3. Sprinkle some cypress leaves on the hot coal.
4. Focus your awareness on your heart chakra and hold your phoenix stone against it.
5. Recite:
   "I am here. I am connected. I am ready."
6. Invite the power of the phoenix and the elemental magic of fire to activate by reciting:
   "I call on the power of the phoenix to connect with me. Heal me. Transform me. Help me to rise up into a new version of myself. So may it be."
7. Pull a Tarot card for an encouraging message.
8. Write down your experiences in your journal or grimoire.
9. Blow out the candle.

CHARGE YOUR WAND

A wand is a tool that serves as an extension of your own will. Cleanse, claim and charge your new wand before using it for ritualistic magic.

You will need:

★ A wand
★ A candle
★ A charcoal disc
★ A cauldron
★ Herbs: rosemary, mugwort, sage
★ The sun
★ Tarot cards: the Magician, the Sun, the Star and the Moon

THE SPELL

1. Lay your wand on your altar.
2. Light the candle.
3. Light the charcoal disc and place it in your cauldron.
4. Sprinkle your cleansing herb on the hot coal and wash the wand with the smoke.
5. Recite:
   "I cleanse my wand of any psychic dissonance or energy that is not serving. I now claim this wand as belonging to me. My wand will serve for the purpose of the higher good."
6. Move to a place where you have access to the sun. This could be in a room with a window or your garden.
7. Hold your wand up to the sun and invite its power to charge your wand by reciting:
   "I call on the power of the sun, the element of fire and my plant allies to activate and charge my wand. So may it be."
8. Return your wand to your altar, placing it vertically. Put the Star card on top, the Magician card below, the Moon card to the left and the Sun card to the right.
9. Blow out the candle.

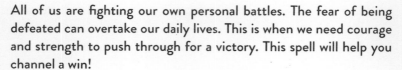

ATTRACT VICTORY

All of us are fighting our own personal battles. The fear of being defeated can overtake our daily lives. This is when we need courage and strength to push through for a victory. This spell will help you channel a win!

△

You will need:

★ A candle
★ A pen and paper
★ A charcoal disc
★ A cauldron
★ Herbs: bay leaf, rose, mint
★ A fan or feather
★ The sun
★ A Tarot card: the Six of Wands

THE SPELL

1. Light the candle.
2. Write down where you want victory in your life on a piece of paper. Fold the paper.
3. Light the charcoal disc and place it in your cauldron.
4. Sprinkle some of your herbal victory blend on the hot coal and move the smoke over the folded paper with a fan or feather.
5. Recite:
   "I banish defeat and I activate victory."
6. Move to a place where you have access to the sun. This could be in a room with a window or your garden.
7. Hold your folded paper up to the sun and recite:
   "I call on the power of the sun, the element of fire and my plant allies to initiate a victory. Victory is mine. So may it be."
8. Return your folded paper to your altar and place the Six of Wands card on top.
9. Blow out the candle.

BANISH ENEMIES

Sadly, some people turn against us and want to do us harm. It's important to have healthy boundaries, but if someone continuously disrespects these boundaries, it's time for a bit of self-defence. This spell will help you to protect your sphere and banish those who wish you harm.

You will need:

- ★ A candle
- ★ A pen and paper
- ★ A charcoal disc
- ★ A cauldron
- ★ Herbs: agrimony, ague, angelica, basil, birch
- ★ A fan or feather
- ★ The sun
- ★ Tarot cards

THE SPELL

1. Light the candle.
2. Meditate on your enemy and send them love.
3. Visualize a circle of fire protecting you.
4. Write down the name of your enemy on a piece of paper and then fold it.
5. Light the charcoal disc and place it in your cauldron.
6. Sprinkle some of your herbal blend on the hot coal and move the smoke over the folded paper with a fan or feather.
7. Recite:
   "I banish my enemy. May I be protected and my boundaries strong."
8. Light the folded paper and place it in your cauldron.
9. Recite:
   "I call on the power of the sun, the element of fire and my plant allies to protect me and keep my enemy away. So may it be."
10. Pull a Tarot card for guidance.
11. Blow out the candle.

BANISH FEAR

Fear impacts all of us. Whether it's fear of the unknown, fear of relationships or fear of failure, here is a spell to help banish fear so you can move forward with courage.

△

You will need:

★ A candle
★ A pen and paper
★ A charcoal disc
★ A cauldron
★ Herbs: chamomile, lavender, thyme
★ A fan or feather
★ The sun
★ Tarot cards

THE SPELL

1. Light the candle.
2. Meditate on your fear and send it love.
3. Write down your fear on a piece of paper. Fold the paper.
4. Light the charcoal disc and place it in your cauldron.
5. Sprinkle some of your herbal blend on the hot coal and move the smoke over the folded paper with a fan or feather.
6. Recite:
   "I banish my fear. I am empowered. I am courageous."
7. Light the folded paper with the candle flame and place it in your cauldron.
8. Recite:
   "I call on the power of the sun, the element of fire and my plant allies to eliminate my fear and replace it with love and courage. So may it be."
9. Pull a Tarot card for guidance.
10. Blow out the candle.

BANISH NIGHTMARES

Bad dreams are no fun! We can learn from our nightmares – they give us clues about where we need to heal in our lives – but they can also disrupt our sleep. Here is a spell to get a good night's sleep.

You will need:

- ★ A candle
- ★ A pen and paper
- ★ A charcoal disc
- ★ A cauldron
- ★ Herbs: angelica, anise, hyssop, rosemary, thyme, burdock
- ★ A fan or feather
- ★ The sun
- ★ Tarot cards

THE SPELL

1. Light the candle.
2. Meditate on your nightmare and send it love.
3. Write down your nightmare on a piece of paper. Fold the paper.
4. Light the charcoal disc and place it in your cauldron.
5. Sprinkle some of your herbal blend on the hot coal and move the smoke over the folded paper with a fan or feather.
6. Recite:
   "I banish my nightmare. I am empowered. I am whole."
7. Light the folded paper with the candle flame and place it in your cauldron.
8. Recite:
   "I call on the power of the sun, the element of fire and my plant allies to banish my nightmare and replace it with healing and love. So may it be."
9. Pull a Tarot card for guidance.
10. Blow out the candle.

FIRE SHIELD

Life can sometimes be overwhelming. This spell can have you feeling protected from the overwhelming energies in no time.

THE SPELL

1. Recite:

   "I call on fire from the south to move to me now."

2. Envision streams of fire moving toward you.

3. Recite:

   "I create a shield of fire around me now. I am safe and protected within its boundaries and no negative energy can penetrate it. So may it be."

 # RING OF FIRE

We always lock our front doors when we go out. You can also energetically protect their homes from any location with this spell.

THE SPELL

1. Recite:

   "I call on fire from the south to move to me now."

2. Envision streams of fire moving toward you.

3. Recite:

   "I create a ring of fire around my home. It is safe and protected. No negative energy can penetrate it. So may it be."

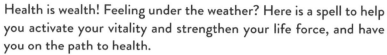

VITALITY

Health is wealth! Feeling under the weather? Here is a spell to help you activate your vitality and strengthen your life force, and have you on the path to health.

You will need:

★ The sun
★ Your phone

THE SPELL

1. Focus your awareness on the sun.
2. Close your eyes and feel the warmth and energy of the sun.
3. Recite:
   "I am here. I am alive. Thank you, sun."
4. Envision yourself healthy and vital.
5. Recite:
   "I call in the power of the sun and the element of fire to bring vitality and good health into my life. So may it be."
6. Take a selfie.
7. Send yourself the photo with the words: "I am healthy. So may it be".

BANISH OBSTACLES

Setbacks and obstacles prevent us from reaching our goals. Here is a banishing spell to help remove those frustrating blocks so your life can flow.

You will need:
- ★ A candle
- ★ A crystal: moldavite
- ★ A pen and paper
- ★ A charcoal disc
- ★ A cauldron
- ★ Herbs: rue, rowan, rosemary
- ★ A fan or feather
- ★ The sun
- ★ Tarot cards

THE SPELL

1. Light the candle.
2. Holding the crystal, meditate on seeing your obstacles vanish.
3. On a piece of paper, write the words: "I banish my obstacles". Fold the paper.
4. Light the charcoal disc and place it in your cauldron.
5. Sprinkle some of your herbal blend on the hot coal and move the smoke over the folded paper with a fan or feather.
6. Recite:
   "I banish my obstacles. They are no more."
7. Light the folded paper with the candle flame and place it in your cauldron.
8. Recite:
   "I call on the power of the sun, the element of fire and my plant allies to banish my obstacles and bring the flow of life. So may it be."
9. Pull a Tarot card for guidance.
10. Blow out the candle.

SEVEN OF WANDS

There are times in life where we need to stand our ground. The Seven of Wands invites us to persevere through external storms and access our inner power. Cast this Tarot spell to activate your self-empowerment.

You will need:

★ A candle
★ A charcoal disc
★ A cauldron
★ A Tarot card: the Seven of Wands
★ A sunflower
★ A fan or feather

THE SPELL

1. Light the candle.
2. Light the charcoal disc and place it in your cauldron.
3. Place the Seven of Wands card in front of you.
4. Close your eyes and set an intention to persevere through the challenges.
5. Envision yourself as the character on the card. Witness as the scene transforms into something more positive.
6. Sprinkle some sunflower on the hot coal and move the smoke over the card with a fan or feather.
7. Recite:
   "I call on the element of fire to activate my empowerment to navigate [name the issue]. So may it be."
8. Blow out the candle.

ACTIVATE SELF-ASSERTION

Sometimes we need to stand up for ourselves, but don't for fear of confrontation. Here is a spell to help make you more assertive in social situations.

△

THE SPELL

1. Recite:
   "I call on fire from the south to move quickly to me now."
2. Envision streams of fire moving toward you.
3. Recite:
   "I activate the power within me to self-assert. I will take action. So may it be."

RAGS TO RICHES

Sometimes we find ourselves skint and in need of money, fast! Here is a spell to invite financial abundance.

△

You will need:

★ The sun
★ A coin
★ Your phone

THE SPELL

1. Focus your awareness on the sun.
2. Close your eyes and feel the warmth and energy of the sun.
3. Recite:
   "I am here. I am alive. Thank you, sun."
4. Hold the coin in your hand and hold it up to the sun.

5. Envision the coin multiplying into thousands of coins.
6. Recite:
   "I call on the power of the sun and the element of fire to bring me money. So may it be."
7. Take a photo of the coin held up to the sun.
8. Send yourself the photo with the words: "I am abundant. So may it be".

  # BANISH AN EX

Sadly, some relationships don't work out. If an ex-partner is not letting go, here is a spell that can help them stay away.

△

THE SPELL

1. Recite:
   "I call on fire from the south to move quickly to me now."
2. Envision streams of fire moving toward you, creating a strong boundary.
3. Recite:
   "I create strong boundaries around me. [Name of ex], stay away. So may it be."

HOT LUCK

Running out of luck? Use this spell to dispel bad luck and invite good fortune.

You will need:

★ A candle
★ The sun
★ A pen and paper
★ A pin
★ Your phone

THE SPELL

1. Light the candle.
2. Close your eyes and feel the warmth and energy of the sun.
3. Recite:
   "I am here. I am alive. Thank you, sun."
4. Focus your awareness on your bout of bad luck and let it go to the light of the sun.
5. On the a piece of paper, write down the words: "Bad luck, be gone".
6. Fold the paper and mark it with the symbol of the sun.
7. Use the candle to melt wax onto the folded paper. With the pin, carve the symbol of the sun into the wax.
8. Let it set and harden.
9. Recite:
   "I call on the power of the sun and the element of fire to bind this bad luck. Initiate good luck into my life with synchronicity and flow. So may it be."
10. Take a photo of the wax-sealed paper and send it to yourself with the words: "Hot luck. So may it be".
11. Blow out the candle.

ALCHEMY INITIATION

The act of inner transformation is the power of alchemy. There are times in life when we feel as though we need to embrace deep inner work, which may entail shadow work and integration, to free us from self-destructive paths. Here is a spell to initiate alchemy in your spiritual path.

You will need:

★ A candle
★ A crystal: labradorite
★ A pen and paper
★ A charcoal disc
★ A cauldron
★ Burdock
★ A fan or feather
★ Tarot cards

THE SPELL

1. Light the candle.
2. Holding the crystal, meditate on seeing your fears dissolving.
3. On a piece of paper, write down the words: "I initiate alchemy in my life". Fold the paper.
4. Light the charcoal disc and place it in your cauldron.
5. Sprinkle some burdock on the hot coal and move the smoke over the folded paper with a fan or feather.
6. Recite:
   "I step out of fear. I initiate alchemy in my life."
7. Put your folded paper on your altar. Place the Judgement card on top of the paper.
8. Recite:
   "I call on the element of fire and my plant allies to initiate my alchemical path for my higher good. So may it be."
9. Pull a Tarot card for an insightful message.
10. Blow out the candle.

FREEDOM IS YOURS!

Do you feel trapped or constrained by another person's energy? It could be in social situations, at work or in a relationship. Here is a spell to help break free.

△

THE SPELL

1. Recite:
   "I call on fire from the south to move quickly to me now."
2. Envision streams of fire moving toward you.
3. Recite:
   "I burn away this imposing energy. I create space. I create freedom. I am liberated. So may it be."

SAY GOODBYE TO THE CLOUDS

The sun boosts mood and positivity. Cast this spell to invite the sun's uplifting rays. Remember when doing weather spells to be responsible. When you effect change in your area, it might have knock-on effects elsewhere. One rule of thumb is to send the clouds to an area that needs it.

△

THE SPELL

1. Focus your awareness on the present moment.
2. Close your eyes.

3. Recite:

"I call on the element of fire from the south to dissipate the clouds and bring sunshine to this area. So may it be."

WARMER TEMPERATURE

It's not fun when we are outdoors and feeling cold. This spell is for when you need to be outside for an extended period of time, and want to invite warmer weather. Remember when doing weather spells to be responsible. Know that when you effect change in your area, it might have knock-on effects elsewhere. One rule of thumb is to send the cold temperature to an area that needs it.

THE SPELL

1. Focus your awareness on the present moment.

2. Close your eyes.

3. Recite:

"I call on the element of fire from the south to move swiftly to send away the cold temperature to [name area] and bring warmer temperatures here. So may it be."

CONNECT TO LIFE PURPOSE

Sometimes we can feel disconnected from our passions, or life purpose. Here is a spell to help you connect!

△

You will need:

★ A candle
★ A crystal: citrine
★ A pen and paper
★ A charcoal disc
★ A cauldron
★ Gum: dammar
★ A fan or feather
★ Tarot cards

THE SPELL

1. Light the candle.
2. Holding the crystal, meditate on connecting to your life purpose.
3. On a piece of paper, write down the words: "I activate my life purpose". Fold the paper.
4. Light the charcoal disc and place it in your cauldron.
5. Place some dammar gum on the hot coal.
6. Move the smoke of the dammar gum over the folded paper with a fan or feather.
7. Recite:
   "I step out of self-limiting beliefs.
   I activate my life purpose."
8. Put your folded paper on your altar. Place the crystal on top of the paper.
9. Recite:
   "I call on the element of fire and my plant allies
   to activate my life purpose. So may it be."
10. Pull a Tarot card for an insightful message.
11. Blow out the candle.

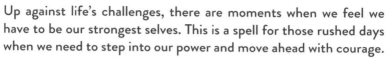

ACTIVATE COURAGE

Up against life's challenges, there are moments when we feel we have to be our strongest selves. This is a spell for those rushed days when we need to step into our power and move ahead with courage.

△

You will need:

★ The sun
★ Your phone
★ A Tarot card: Strength

THE SPELL

1. Focus your awareness on the sun.
2. Close your eyes and feel the warmth and energy of the sun.
3. Recite:
   "I am here. I am alive. Thank you, sun."
4. Envision yourself being filled with powerful light.
5. Recite:
   "I call on the power of the sun and the element of fire to fill me with courage."
6. Send yourself a photo of the Strength card with the words: "I have courage".

FIRE SCRYING

Scrying is the ancient art of seeing messages when gazing into a surface, such as a mirror, pool of water or crystal. Scrying can also be done with fire. Here is a spell that employs scrying to invite insights.

△

You will need:

★ A candle
★ A pen and paper
★ A charcoal disc
★ A cauldron
★ Yarrow
★ A fan or feather

THE SPELL

1. Light the candle.
2. On a piece of paper, write the words: "I activate fire scrying". Fold the paper.
3. Light the charcoal disc and place it in your cauldron.
4. Sprinkle yarrow on the hot coal and move the smoke over the paper with a fan or feather.
5. Recite:
   "I activate fire scrying and the ability to divine through fire."
6. Put the folded paper on your altar with some yarrow on top.
7. Recite:
   "I call on the element of fire and my plant allies to activate my ability to fire scry. So may it be."
8. Breathe deeply and fix your gaze on the flame of your candle as it flickers.
9. Open your mind to any thoughts and images.
10. After 10–15 minutes, return your awareness to the room you are in.
11. Blow out the candle.

A CANDLE DIVINATION

This spell is only helpful if you know how to fire scry. If you don't know how to yet, I would recommend doing the Fire Scrying Spell first (see page 136)! This candle divination spell will help you receive some guidance.

△

You will need:

★ A candle

THE SPELL

1. Light the candle.
2. Take some time to observe and connect with the flame.
3. Recite:

   "I call on the power of fire to bring me guidance. So may it be."
4. Breathe deeply and relax as you fix your gaze on the flame of your candle. Watch the flame flicker and flash.
5. Ask the flame your question:

   "Oh, fire, what should I do about [name issue]?"
6. Open your mind to any thoughts and images that appear.
7. After 10–15 minutes, return your awareness to the room you are in.
8. Blow out the candle.

THIRD EYE ACTIVATION

Our third eye provides perception beyond ordinary sight. It is often associated with clairvoyant abilities: clear seeing and the power to see the future, the past and other mystical phenomena. Cast this spell to connect with your inner vision.

△

You will need:

★ A candle
★ A charcoal disc
★ A cauldron
★ Lavender
★ A fan or feather
★ A crystal: amethyst

THE SPELL

1. Light the candle.
2. Light the charcoal disc and place it in your cauldron.
3. Sprinkle lavender on the hot coal and move the smoke over your forehead with a fan or feather.
4. Recite:
   "I unblock all obstacles and activate my third eye."
5. Lie down and place the crystal on your forehead between your eyes.
6. Recite:
   "I call on the power of the element of fire to activate my ability to see. Open my third eye. May it be so."
7. Breathe deeply and bring your awareness to the place behind your closed eyes.
8. Open your mind to any thoughts and images that appear.
9. After 10–15 minutes, return your awareness to the room you are in.
10. Blow out the candle.

SEX MAGIC

Erotic energy has been used in spellcrafting for hundreds of years. Sexual energy is life force energy intrinsically connected to creation. When an orgasm is directed toward an intention, it can manifest an outcome quickly! This manifestation spell doubles as self-care!

You will need:

- ★ A candle
- ★ A charcoal disc
- ★ A cauldron
- ★ A pen and paper
- ★ Rose petals
- ★ A fan or feather
- ★ A crystal: rose quartz

THE SPELL

1. Light the candle.
2. Light the charcoal disc and place it in your cauldron.
3. Close your eyes and connect to your intention.
4. Write your intention on a piece of paper, then fold the paper and put it on your altar.
5. Place some rose petals on the hot coal and move the smoke over the paper with a fan or feather.
6. Place the crystal on top of the paper.
7. Recite:
   "I call on the element of fire to move through my body. So may it be."
8. Close your eyes and self-pleasure to the point of orgasm.
9. As you orgasm, direct your focus on your intention.
10. Recite:
    "I manifest [name your intention]. So may it be!"
11. Blow out the candle.

TWIN FLAME

The connection with a twin flame is deep! When you meet this person there is a strong sense of recognition and attraction. The bond is spiritual and will pull you through great spiritual transformations. If you are ready for that journey with another person, this spell could be for you.

You will need:

★ A candle
★ A knife
★ An apple
★ Saffron
★ A ribbon
★ Small pins

THE SPELL

1. Light the candle.
2. Cut the apple in half.
3. Carve the number 11 on the outside of both halves.
4. Make a small hole on the inside of both halves.
5. Sprinkle the saffron into both of the hollows.
6. Push the halves together, making the apple whole again, and bind it together with ribbon and pins.
7. Close your eyes and connect to your intention.
8. Recite:
   "I call on the element of fire to connect me to my twin flame. So may it be."
9. Blow out the candle.

ATTRACT A NEW FRIEND

Feel in need of a new friend? Something within you is yearning and knows they are out there. Here is a spell for welcoming that new connection!

△

You will need:

★ A candle
★ Tulip petals
★ A small pouch

THE SPELL

1. Light the candle.
2. Place the tulip petals in the small pouch.
3. Hold the pouch in your hands. Close your eyes.
4. Feel the warmth and the brightness of the flame on your eyelids.
5. Envision yourself and the pouch being filled with powerful light.
6. Recite:

   "I call on the element of fire to bring me a new friend. So may it be."

7. Blow out the candle.
8. Carry your tulip pouch around with you in your bag.

BANISH JEALOUSY

The green-eyed monster! Jealousy never feels good, but it is rooted in fear. Here is a spell to help cast away its negative effects.

You will need:

★ A candle
★ A charcoal disc
★ A cauldron
★ Holly leaves
★ Rose petals
★ Small pouch

THE SPELL

1. Light the candle.
2. Light the charcoal disc and place it in your cauldron.
3. Close your eyes and focus on your jealousy.
4. Sprinkle some holly leaves and rose petals on the hot coal and use the smoke to cleanse yourself.
5. Recite:
   "I call on the element of fire to burn away my jealousy. So may it be."
6. Place the remaining holly and rose in the small pouch.
7. Hold the pouch and close your eyes.
8. Feel the warmth and the brightness of the flame on your eyelids.
9. Envision yourself and the pouch being filled with powerful light
10. Recite:
    "I am free of jealousy. So may it be."
11. Blow out the candle.
12. Carry your pouch around with you in your bag.

CORD CUTTING

After a relationship has ended, it is often necessary to cut energetic cords that keep us tethered to the person. Here is a spell to help you move on and keep your energy healthy.

You will need:

★ A candle
★ A crystal: black obsidian

THE SPELL

1. Light the candle.
2. Hold the crystal in your hand.
3. Relax into your mediation and feel the warmth and the brightness of the flame on your eyelids.
4. Envision yourself and the crystal being filled with powerful light.
5. Visualize the energetic cord connected to the other person.
6. Use your crystal to begin cutting the cord.
7. Recite:
   "Through the power of the element of fire I cut the cord connected to [name the person] and I call my energy back from them. So may it be."
8. Picture your energy coming back to you from the person.
9. Blow out the candle.

PHYSICAL STAMINA

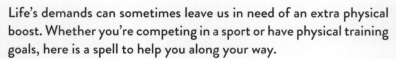

Life's demands can sometimes leave us in need of an extra physical boost. Whether you're competing in a sport or have physical training goals, here is a spell to help you along your way.

△

You will need:

★ A candle
★ A knife
★ Ginger root
★ Small pouch

THE SPELL

1. Light the candle.
2. Carve the symbol for fire into your ginger root.
3. Hold the root of ginger in your hand.
4. Close your eyes and feel the warmth and the brightness of the flame on your eyelids.
5. Envision yourself and the ginger root being filled with powerful light.
6. Recite:
   "I call on the element of fire to bring me stamina for [name the reason]. So may it be."
7. Blow out the candle.
8. Carry your ginger root pouch around with you in your bag.

REVERSE A CURSE

Have you ever felt that you've been cursed? Something just doesn't feel right and your intuition is letting you know that things are amiss. Here is a spell to reverse a curse and make you feel much better.

You will need:

- ★ Salt
- ★ Wormwood
- ★ Pestle and mortar
- ★ Small mirror
- ★ A sprig of rosemary
- ★ A candle

THE SPELL

1. Grind the salt and the wormwood together with your pestle and mortar.
2. Lay the small mirror on your altar and the sprig of rosemary to its side.
3. Light the candle.
4. Sprinkle the herbal mixture around the mirror.
5. Close your eyes and feel the warmth and the brightness of the flame on your eyelids.
6. Envision yourself being filled with powerful light.
7. Visualize the energy of the curse reflecting onto the mirror and bouncing away from you.
8. Recite:

   "I call on the element of fire to reverse this curse away from me. I am protected and at peace. So may it be."

9. Light the sprig of rosemary and cleanse your mirror with the smoke.
10. Blow out the candle.

BANISH A BAD TEMPER

A fiery temper can be a repeat problem for some folks and often leads to regret. Here is a spell to help bind the tendency toward anger, and to call in patience.

△

You will need:

★ A candle
★ A knife
★ A chilli pepper
★ A ribbon

THE SPELL

1. Light the candle.
2. With your knife, carve the symbol for fire into your chilli pepper.
3. Hold the chilli pepper in your hand.
4. Close your eyes and feel the warmth and the brightness of the flame on your eyelids.
5. Envision yourself and the chilli being filled with powerful light.
6. Recite:
   "I call on the element of fire to bind my temper and bring empowerment. So may it be."
7. Bind the chilli pepper with the ribbon.
8. Place it on your altar.
9. Blow out the candle.

SPEED UP HEALING

Getting ill is never fun! Here is a spell to expedite your healing.

△

You will need:

★ A candle
★ A knife
★ A garlic bulb
★ A needle and thread

THE SPELL

1. Light the candle.
2. With your knife, carve the symbol for fire into your garlic bulb.
3. Thread the needle.
4. Push the threaded needle through the garlic bulb. Once it is all the way through, cut it away from the needle and tie a knot on the end. Your garlic bulb should now be hanging from the thread.
5. Close your eyes and feel the warmth and the brightness of the flame on your eyelids.
6. Envision yourself and the garlic bulb being filled with powerful light.
7. Recite:
   "I call on the element of fire to speed up my healing from [name the reason]. So may it be."
8. Hang your bulb of garlic somewhere on your altar.
9. Blow out the candle.

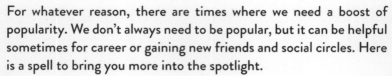

POPULARITY BOOSTER

For whatever reason, there are times where we need a boost of popularity. We don't always need to be popular, but it can be helpful sometimes for career or gaining new friends and social circles. Here is a spell to bring you more into the spotlight.

△

You will need:

★ A knife
★ An orange
★ A bowl
★ Basil
★ A candle

THE SPELL

1. Cut a hole in the top of the orange.
2. Carve the symbol for fire on the side of the orange.
3. Place the orange in the bowl.
4. Sprinkle basil into the hole atop the orange, and then push the candle in the hole.
5. Light the candle.
6. Close your eyes and feel the warmth and the brightness of the flame on your eyelids.
7. Envision yourself being filled with powerful light and joy.
8. Visualize yourself becoming popular.
9. Recite:
   "I call on the element of fire to bring me popularity. So may it be."
10. Allow the candle to burn all the way down.

GOOD HEALTH

Good health entails living a healthy lifestyle, balancing the needs of mind, body and spirit. Use this sigil spell to help maintain your commitment to the greatest wealth of all: health.

△

You will need:

★ A candle
★ A pen and paper
★ A crystal: red jasper

THE SPELL

1. Light the candle.
2. Prepare your sigil: you will be using the words "Good health". Drop the vowels and any duplicate letters so you end up with: "G D H L T". Re-write these letters on your piece of paper, arranging them in a creative way, and add these symbols: ♥ 🔥
3. Hold your sigil.
4. Close your eyes and feel the warmth of the fire moving within you.
5. Envision yourself and the sigil filled with powerful light.
6. Recite:
   "I call on the element of fire to bring good health into my life. So may it be."
7. Place your sigil on your altar. Put the crystal on top of the sigil.
8. Blow out the candle.

⟨E⟩ ACE OF WANDS

Have you ever had one of those days where you feel stuck in a rut? The Ace of Wands is here to help. This Tarot card is charged with energy that invites new opportunities, inspiration, growth and potential. Cast this spell to activate a new chapter!

△

You will need:

★ A Tarot card: the Ace of Wands

★ Your phone

THE SPELL

1. Place the Ace of Wands card in front of you.
2. Close your eyes and focus your awareness on the inspired action of the card.
3. Feel the excitement of new possibilities being activated in your life.
4. Recite:
   "I call on the element of fire to bring me new opportunities. So may it be."
5. Send yourself an image of the Ace of Wands card with the words: "I attract new opportunities".

TRANSFORM SADNESS

Sometimes life can bring us down. These are times for more self-care and self-compassion. Here is a sigil spell to blow away negativity, connect with your heart and transform your sadness into joy.

△

You will need:

★ A candle
★ A pen and paper
★ A cauldron

THE SPELL

1. Light the candle.
2. Prepare your sigil: you will be using the word: "Sadness". Drop the vowels and any duplicate letters so you end up with: "S D N". Re-write these letters on your piece of paper, arranging them in a creative way, and add the symbol for fire.
3. Hold your sigil.
4. Close your eyes and feel the warmth moving within you.
5. Envision yourself and the sigil filled with powerful light.
6. Recite:
   "I call on the element of fire to transform my sadness and bring me joy. So may it be."
7. Put your sigil in the candle flame and light it.
8. Place the burning sigil in the cauldron and let it burn to ash.
9. Blow out the candle.

INCREASE CREATIVE FLOW

Sometimes we can experience creative blocks. Here is a spell to help the creative juices flow again!

You will need:
★ Your phone

THE SPELL

1. Search for an image of your creative tool on your phone. For example, if you are a musician, it could be a guitar.
2. Close your eyes and feel the warmth and positivity of creating.
3. Recite:
   "I call on the element of fire to increase my creativity. So may it be."
4. Send yourself this image with the words: "I attract good vibes".

INTENSIFY LOVE

So you wish to deepen your love? This spell will help turn a crush into something more.

You will need:
★ Your phone

THE SPELL

1. Find an image of your crush on your phone.
2. Close your eyes and focus your awareness on your love for them.
3. Feel the warmth and positivity of that love deepening.

4. Recite:

   "I call on the element of fire to intensify the love between [name your crush] and I. So may it be."

5. Send yourself the image with the words: "Intensify love".

ACTIVATE A CREATIVE PROJECT

The potential energy around a creative project can be potent. Bringing that potential into fruition, however, is another matter. This spell will help to nurture the seed of an idea so it manifests as you imagine it.

△

You will need:

★ A pen and paper

★ Your phone

THE SPELL

1. Write down or draw your idea on a piece of paper.

2. Hold the paper and close your eyes.

3. Focus your awareness on the positive feelings of your project manifesting.

4. Recite:

   "I call on the element of fire to activate my creative project. So may it be."

5. Send yourself a photo of your piece of paper with the words: "I manifest this".

BIND COMPETITIVE BEHAVIOUR

Competitive behaviour can create unwanted drama. It can become an obstacle when trying to achieve balance and happiness in life. This competitiveness can come from within ourselves or from others. Here is a spell to reduce the drama!

△

You will need:

★ A candle
★ A pen and paper
★ A ribbon

THE SPELL

1. Light the candle.
2. Prepare your sigil: you will be using the word: "Competition". Drop the vowels and any duplicate letters so you end up with: "C M P T N". Re-write these letters on your piece of paper, arranging them in a creative way, and add the symbol for fire.
3. Hold your sigil.
4. Close your eyes and feel the warmth of the fire moving within you.
5. Envision yourself and the sigil filled with powerful light.
6. Recite:
   "I call on the element of fire to bind competitive behaviour. So may it be."
7. Bind your sigil by wrapping the ribbon around it.
8. Place your bound sigil on your altar.
9. Blow out the candle.

(E) BANISH SHYNESS

Being shy can be stressful in social situations. It can also prevent us from forming new friendships and meaningful connections with others. This tech spell will help you banish your shyness, opening up new possibilities.

△

You will need:

★ Your phone

THE SPELL

1. Take a selfie.
2. Close your eyes and focus your awareness on the image.
3. Feel love, self-compassion and joy for yourself.
4. Envision fire energy moving through you, bringing confidence.
5. Recite:
   "I call on the element of fire to banish my shyness and bring me confidence. So may it be."
6. Send yourself the selfie with the words: "I am confident".

BANISH PROCRASTINATION

Procrastination is a form of self-sabotage. Cast this spell to get you back onto the path of productivity and personal growth.

You will need:

★ A candle
★ A pen and paper
★ A cauldron

THE SPELL

1. Light the candle.
2. Prepare your sigil: you will be using the word: "Procrastination". Drop the vowels and any duplicate letters so you end up with: "P R C S T N". Re-write these letters on your piece of paper, arranging them in a creative way, and add the symbol for fire.
3. Hold your sigil.
4. Close your eyes and feel the warmth moving within you.
5. Envision yourself and the sigil filled with powerful light.
6. Recite:
   "I call on the element of fire to banish my procrastination and bring productivity. So may it be."
7. Put your sigil in the candle flame and light it.
8. Place the burning sigil in the cauldron and let it burn to ash.
9. Blow out the candle.

⊛ CAMPFIRE RELEASE

Campfires are associated with camping trips and being outdoors. The campfire is, however, ancient and primal, serving as a place of survival, community, warmth and nourishment. Here is a spell to cast the next time you are on a camping trip, to release anything holding you back and to reconnect with the heart.

△

You will need:

★ An object from nature: i.e. a piece of wood, pinecone, or leaf
★ A campfire

THE SPELL

1. Hold the natural object in your hand.
2. Close your eyes and feel the campfire warming your eyelids.
3. Envision yourself being filled with powerful light.
4. Visualize the negative issues you want to burn away moving into the natural object in your hand.
5. Recite:

   "I call on the element of fire to burn away [name the issue]. I am free. So may it be."
6. Throw the object into the campfire to burn.

⊛ PICK-ME-UP

Try this spell when you are feeling tired and need an energy boost.

△

You will need:

★ Your phone

THE SPELL

1. Close your eyes and set an intention to become more alert.
2. Envision the element of fire moving toward you and activating energy.
3. Recite:
   "I call on the element of fire to wake me up. So may it be."
4. Send yourself a digital sigil with your initials and the lightning emoji. Your sigil should look something like this: T ⚡ C.

 ⊛ ACTIVATE MOTIVATION

We all have lazy days! But sometimes life is demanding and we need to get back to work. Here is a spell to get you feeling more motivated.

△

You will need:

★ A Tarot card: the Chariot
★ Your phone

THE SPELL

1. Place the Chariot card in front of you.
2. Close your eyes and focus your awareness on the power of the Chariot card.

3. Envision yourself as the Chariot rider, full of determination and power.

4. Recite:

   "I call on the element of fire to activate my motivation. So may it be."

5. Send yourself an image of the Chariot card with the words: "I am motivated. I am determined."

✦ ⟨E⟩ MAKE A WISH ON A FIREFLY

Fireflies bring twinkling magic to gardens. Their appearance can feel surprising and mystical and bring about positivity and joy. They are also great symbols of hope and inspiration. Next time you see a firefly, cast this wish spell.

You will need:

★ A firefly

THE SPELL

1. Spot the firefly.

2. Close your eyes and envision the element of fire moving through you.

3. Connect to the inspirational magic of the firefly.

4. Set an intention.

5. Recite:

   "I call on the element of fire to grant my wish to [name the wish]. So may it be."

CONNECT WITH YOUR
SALAMANDER GUIDE

The salamander is a powerful fire elemental entity. When called into our lives, salamander guides bring great magical change and healing. The word "salamander" comes from the Greek word for fireplace, *salambe*, and although they can be mistaken for water elementals, living in watery areas, they resonate with fire. Here is a spell to help you connect to your salamander guide.

You will need:
- ★ A candle
- ★ Your phone
- ★ A charcoal disc
- ★ A cauldron
- ★ Saffron

THE SPELL

1. Light the candle.
2. Search for an image of a salamander on your phone.
3. Light the charcoal disc and place it in your cauldron.
4. Close your eyes and focus your awareness on the image of the salamander.
5. Feel the warmth and positivity of connecting to the salamander guide.
6. Sprinkle some saffron on the hot coal.
7. Recite:
   "I call on the element of fire to bring connection with my salamander guide. So may it be."
8. Sit in quiet meditation.
9. Send yourself the image of the salamander with the words: "My guide".
10. Blow out the candle.

⟨E⟩ MAKE ME FAMOUS

Some people were born for fame. Perhaps you are one of them! Whatever you seek fame for, cast this spell to get the ball rolling. This spell should be done mindfully: fame comes with consequences, both positive and negative.

△

You will need:

★ Your phone

THE SPELL

1. Take a selfie.
2. Close your eyes and focus your awareness on the image.
3. Feel love, self-compassion and joy for yourself.
4. Make a positive affirmation for your fame to have positive effects.
5. Envision thousands of golden souls flying in toward your image.
6. Recite:

   "I call on the element of fire to bring me fame. So may it be."

7. Post your selfie on social media with the crystal ball, star and heart emojis.

⟨E⟩ LEADERSHIP SPELL

The responsibility of leadership, whether at work or in family life, can be challenging but also rewarding. Here is a spell to help strengthen leadership.

△

You will need:

★ A Tarot card: the Emperor
★ Your phone

THE SPELL

1. Place the Emperor card in front of you.
2. Close your eyes and focus your awareness on the power of the Emperor.
3. Envision yourself as the Emperor, full of determination and power.
4. Recite:
   "I call on the element of fire to activate my leadership. So may it be."
5. Send yourself an image of the Emperor card with the words: "I step into my leadership".

  ⟨E⟩ HOT DATE

Have you been patiently waiting for your crush to ask you out? Try this spell on the go to manifest a hot date with your crush.

△

You will need:

★ Your phone

THE SPELL

1. Close your eyes and set an intention to manifest a hot date with your crush.
2. Envision the element of fire moving toward you and activating passion.

3. Recite:

   "I call on the element of fire to activate a hot date with [name your crush]. So may it be."

4. Send yourself a digital sigil with the initials of your crush and the fire emoji. Your sigil should look something like this: R 🔥 B.

FINANCIAL GROWTH SPELL

We all need money to survive. This spell will help you with financial growth and saving.

You will need:

★ A candle
★ Coins
★ Herbs: cloves, nutmeg, ginger, thyme
★ A small pouch

THE SPELL

1. Light the candle.
2. Prepare your charm bag by adding the coins and herbs to a small pouch.
3. Close the pouch and hold it in your hands.
4. Close your eyes and envision your savings increasing.
5. Recite:

   "I call on the element of fire to grow my finances. So may it be."

6. Blow out the candle.
7. Carry your charm pouch around with you in your bag.

WATER
SPELLS

In elemental magic, water is perfect for spells connected to winter, emotions, creativity, purification, cleansing, initiation, intuition, spiritual abilities, dreams, menstrual cycles, the unconscious, love, relationships, phobias and fears. In each of the water spells, it is important to envision the energy of the water moving through you, contributing its power to your intentions.

NEW MOON IN SCORPIO

The new moon is the perfect time for setting an intention to manifest something. The new moon in Scorpio is an opportunity to call in new energies of transformation, deep intuition and spiritual growth into your life.

You will need:

- ★ A candle
- ★ A charcoal disc
- ★ A cauldron
- ★ A pen and paper
- ★ A Tarot card: Death
- ★ Nettle (dried)

THE SPELL

1. Light the candle.
2. Light the charcoal disc and place it in your cauldron.
3. Focus on your intention and visualize it coming into being.
4. Write your intention on a piece of paper.
5. Fold the paper and place it on your altar. Place the Death card on top of the paper.
6. Recite:

   "I call on the element of water from the west. Move quickly to me and fuel my spell."
7. Sprinkle some nettle on the hot coal.
8. Recite:

   "By the power of the new moon in Scorpio, the Death card and my plant ally, I manifest my intention. So may it be."
9. Blow out the candle.

NEW MOON IN PISCES

The new moon is the perfect time for setting an intention to manifest something new. The new moon in Pisces is an opportunity to call in new energies of imagination, dreams and creativity into your life.

▽

You will need:

★ A candle
★ A charcoal disc
★ A cauldron
★ A pen and paper
★ A Tarot card:
   the Moon
★ Basil

THE SPELL

1. Light the candle.
2. Light the charcoal disc and place it in your cauldron.
3. Focus on your intention and visualize it coming into being.
4. Write your intention on a piece of paper.
5. Fold the paper and put it on your altar. Place the Moon card on top of the paper.
6. Recite:
   "I call on the element of water from the west. Move quickly to me and fuel my spell."
7. Sprinkle some basil on the hot coal.
8. Recite:
   "By the power of the new moon in Pisces, the Moon card and my plant ally, I manifest my intention. So may it be."
9. Blow out the candle.

NEW MOON IN CANCER

The new moon is the perfect time for setting an intention to manifest something new. The new moon in Cancer is an opportunity to call in new energies of personal empowerment and empathy into your life.

▽

You will need:

★ A candle
★ A charcoal disc
★ A cauldron
★ A pen and paper
★ A Tarot card: the Chariot
★ A bay leaf

THE SPELL

1. Light the candle.
2. Light the charcoal disc and place it in your cauldron.
3. Focus on your intention and visualize it coming into being.
4. Write your intention on a piece of paper.
5. Fold the paper and put it on your altar. Place the Chariot card on top of the paper.
6. Recite:

   "I call on the element of water from the west. Move quickly to me and fuel my spell."

7. Put the bay leaf on the hot coal.
8. Recite:

   "By the power of the new moon in Cancer, the Chariot card and my plant ally, I manifest my intention. So may it be."

9. Blow out the candle.

FULL MOON IN SCORPIO

The full moon is the ideal time for letting go of things that no longer serve you. It is an event of great catharsis and wholeness, where emotions from the deep unconscious come up to the light to integrate. The full moon in Scorpio is an opportunity to release energies of obsession, grief and jealousy.

▽

You will need:

★ A candle
★ A charcoal disc
★ A cauldron
★ A pen and paper
★ A fireproof bowl
★ A crystal: green aventurine
★ Nettle (dried)

THE SPELL

1. Light the candle.
2. Light the charcoal disc and place it in your cauldron.
3. Write down what you want to release on a piece of paper.
4. Fold the paper and light it with the candle flame. Put the burning paper in a fireproof bowl and let it burn to ash.
5. Hold the crystal and recite:
   "I call on the element of water from the west. Move quickly to wash away that which no longer serves me."
6. Sprinkle some nettle on the hot coal.
7. Recite:
   "By the power of the full moon in Scorpio, the green aventurine crystal and my plant ally, I set myself free. So may it be."
8. Blow out the candle.

FULL MOON IN PISCES

The full moon is the ideal time for letting go of things that no longer serve you. It is an event of great catharsis and wholeness, where emotions from the deep unconscious come up to the light to integrate. The full moon in Pisces is an opportunity to release energies of self-pity, moodiness and low self-esteem.

▽

You will need:

★ A candle
★ A charcoal disc
★ A cauldron
★ A pen and paper
★ A fireproof bowl
★ A crystal: moonstone
★ Basil

THE SPELL

1. Light the candle.
2. Light the charcoal disc and place it in your cauldron.
3. Focus your awareness on your emotional wellbeing.
4. Write down what you want to release on a piece of paper.
5. Fold the paper and light it in the candle flame. Put the burning paper in a fireproof bowl and let it burn to ash.
6. Hold your crystal and recite:
   "I call on the element of water from the west. Move quickly to wash away that which no longer serves me."
7. Sprinkle some basil on the hot coal.
8. Recite:
   "By the power of the full moon in Pisces, the moonstone and my plant ally, I set myself free. So may it be."
9. Blow out the candle.

FULL MOON IN CANCER

The full moon is the ideal time for letting go of things that no longer serve you. It is an event of great catharsis and wholeness, where emotions from the deep unconscious come up to the light to integrate. The full moon in Cancer is an opportunity to release energies of resentment, anxiety and sadness.

You will need:

★ A candle
★ A charcoal disc
★ A cauldron
★ A pen and paper
★ A fireproof bowl
★ A crystal:
 rose quartz
★ A bay leaf

THE SPELL

1. Light the candle.
2. Light the charcoal disc and place it in your cauldron.
3. Draw awareness to your emotional wellbeing.
4. Write down what you want to release on a piece of paper.
5. Fold the paper and light it in the candle flame. Put the burning paper in a fireproof bowl and let it burn to ash.
6. Hold the crystal and recite:
 "I call on the element of water from the west. Move quickly to wash away that which no longer serves me."
7. Put the bay leaf on the hot coal.
8. Recite:
 "By the power of the full moon in Cancer, the rose quartz crystal and my plant ally, I set myself free. So may it be."
9. Blow out the candle.

SOLAR RETURN SCORPIO

It's your birthday! Birthdays hold potent energy for spellwork. It's time to honour the return of the sun to the natal chart position that you were born in. The solar return in Scorpio is especially potent for stronger life force energy, increased cosmic connections and powerful manifestation potential. Use this spell to create a more intuitive year ahead!

You will need:

★ A candle
★ A charcoal disc
★ A cauldron
★ A pen and paper
★ Nettle (dried)
★ Tarot cards

THE SPELL

1. Light the candle.
2. Light the charcoal disc and place it in your cauldron.
3. Feel gratitude for being alive and give thanks to the sun.
4. Recite:
   "I honour the sun and my life on this day of my solar return. I call on the element of water from the west. Move quickly to activate my purpose and manifest my wishes this coming year."
5. Write down your birthday wishes.
6. Sprinkle some nettle on the hot coal.
7. Recite:
   "By the power of my solar return in Scorpio and my plant ally, I manifest my birthday wishes. So may it be."
8. Pull a Tarot card for your year ahead.
9. Blow out the candle.

SOLAR RETURN PISCES

It's your birthday! Birthdays hold potent energy for spellwork. It's time to honour the return of the sun to the natal chart position that you were born in. The solar return in Pisces an opportunity to manifest a more creative year ahead.

You will need:

★ A candle
★ A charcoal disc
★ A cauldron
★ A pen and paper
★ Basil
★ Tarot cards

THE SPELL

1. Light the candle.
2. Light the charcoal disc and place it in your cauldron.
3. Feel gratitude for being alive and give thanks to the sun.
4. Recite:
   "I honour the sun and my life on this day of my solar return. I call on the element of water from the west. Move quickly to activate my purpose and manifest my wishes this coming year."
5. Write down your birthday wishes.
6. Sprinkle some basil on the hot coal.
7. Recite:
   "By the power of my solar return in Pisces and my plant ally, I manifest my birthday wishes. So may it be."
8. Pull a Tarot card for your year ahead.
9. Blow out the candle.

SOLAR RETURN CANCER

It's your birthday! Birthdays hold potent energy for spellwork. It's time to honour the return of the sun to the natal chart position that you were born in. The solar return in Cancer is especially potent for creating a more loving year ahead.

▽

You will need:

★ A candle
★ A charcoal disc
★ A cauldron
★ A pen and paper
★ Bay leaf
★ Tarot cards

THE SPELL

1. Light the candle.
2. Light the charcoal disc and place it in your cauldron.
3. Feel gratitude for being alive and give thanks to the sun.
4. Recite:

   "I honour the sun and my life on this day of my solar return. I call on the element of water from the west. Move quickly to activate my purpose and manifest my wishes this coming year."

5. Write down your birthday wishes.
6. Put a bay leaf on the hot coal.
7. Recite:

   "By the power of my solar return in Cancer and my plant ally, I manifest my birthday wishes. So may it be."

8. Pull a Tarot card for your year ahead.
9. Blow out the candle.

AUTUMN EQUINOX RELEASE

The autumn equinox, also called the fall equinox, arrives each year between 22 and 23 September in the Northern Hemisphere. It is the perfect time to begin to move inward and let go of areas in your life that need to wither. Cast this spell on the autumn equinox to identify what is no longer working for you and release the past.

You will need:

★ A leaf
★ A marker
★ Access to a body of water

THE SPELL

1. Hold the leaf in your hand.
2. Close your eyes and meditate on what you want to release.
3. Write your intention on the leaf.
4. Recite:
   "I call on the element of water to carry this away and make room for what is new. So may it be."
5. Go outdoors and put the leaf in a river/lake/stream. If you don't have access to a body of water, you can flush your leaf down the toilet.

SAMHAIN SORCERY

Happy Witches' New Year! Samhain falls annually on 31 October. Known by most of the world as Halloween, the veil between worlds is thin during this time, allowing easier access to the spirit world. Cast this spell to reach the other side.

▽

You will need:

★ A candle
★ Offerings: apple, pomegranate, squash, pumpkin
★ A charcoal disc
★ A cauldron
★ Crystals: obsidian, fluorite, smoky quartz, labradorite, hematite
★ A pen and paper
★ A Tarot card: Death
★ Herbs: rosemary, mugwort, rowan, blessed thistle
★ Resin: myrrh
★ Optional: photos of your ancestors or deceased loved ones for your altar

THE SPELL

1. Light the candle.
2. Place your offerings on your altar.
3. Light the charcoal disc and place it in your cauldron.
4. Arrange your crystals in a grid, hold a crystal in your palm or place them on energetic centres of your body.
5. Recite:
   "I call on the element of water from the west and connect to [name the person] with unconditional love and for the higher good."
6. Write down the name of the ancestor or deceased loved one with whom you wish to connect.
7. Fold the piece of paper and put it on your altar with the Death card on top.
8. Sprinkle some of your herbal blend as well as the myrrh on the hot coal.
9. Recite:
   "Through the power of the thinning of the veil, Death and my plant allies, I open communication with you now. So may it be."

10. Allow yourself to sit in meditation, receptive to any insights, messages or energy from the other side.
11. Thank your ancestors.
12. Allow the candle to burn through the night until it goes out. Make sure you can safely leave the candle unattended.

BRING THE RAIN

Continuous dry weather can bring drought, and rain is needed to help revive the earth. Try this spell to invite much-needed showers. Remember to be responsible when casting weather spells. Know that when you effect change in your area that it might have knock-on effects. One rule of thumb is to send the dry weather to an area that needs it.

THE SPELL

1. Focus your awareness on the present moment.
2. Close your eyes.
3. Recite:
   "I call on the element of water from the west to swiftly arrive to quench this drought with some rainfall. So may it be."

CRYSTAL CLEANSING AND CHARGING

Crystals are a magical tool for healing, wellbeing and spiritual support. Use this spell to cleanse your newly acquired crystals.

▽

You will need:

★ A candle
★ A charcoal disc
★ A cauldron
★ Herbs: rosemary, mugwort, frankincense
★ Your newly acquired crystal(s)
★ A fan or feather
★ Salt
★ A bowl of water
★ The full moon
★ Tarot cards: the High Priestess, the Moon, the Star and the Sun

THE SPELL

1. Light the candle.
2. Light the charcoal disc and place it in your cauldron.
3. Sprinkle your herb of choice on the hot coal.
4. Wash the smoke over your crystal using a fan or feather.
5. Recite:
   "I cleanse my crystal of all psychic dissonance and energy that is not serving. I now claim this crystal as belonging to me."
6. Sprinkle salt into the bowl of water and mix.
7. Place your crystal in the bowl and leave in the light of the full moon.
8. Recite:
   "I call on the power of the full moon and the element of water to cleanse and charge my crystal. So may it be."
9. Blow out the candle.
10. The following day, return your crystal to your altar, placing the Moon card above, the High Priestess card below, the Star card to the left and the Sun card to the right.

STOP SELF-DESTRUCTING

Self-destructive behaviour can interfere with your happiness and wellbeing. Use this spell to set yourself free.

You will need:

★ An ice-cube tray
★ Water
★ A candle
★ A pen and paper
★ A charcoal disc
★ A cauldron
★ Herbs: agrimony, ague, angelica, basil
★ A fan or feather
★ Scissors
★ Tarot cards

THE SPELL

1. Fill an ice-cube tray with water.
2. Light the candle.
3. Write down your self-destructive behaviour on a piece of paper. Fold the paper.
4. Light the charcoal disc and place it in your cauldron.
5. Sprinkle the herbs on the hot coal.
6. Move the smoke over the folded paper with a fan or feather.
7. Recite:
   "I cleanse myself of my self-destructive behaviour."
8. Cut the paper up into small pieces and drop these in the water in the ice-cube tray.
9. Recite:
   "I call on the element of water to bind and freeze my self-destructive behaviour. May it be no more. So may it be."
10. Put the ice-cube tray in the freezer.
11. Pull a Tarot card for guidance.
12. Blow out the candle.
13. After 30 days, bury the ice cubes in the earth.

BANISH THE FEAR OF SWIMMING

The fear of water is a real concern for some folks. It can prevent the enjoyment of swimming or even, in some cases, being near water. This spell will help to banish this phobia and bring ease and peace around this element.

You will need:

★ A candle
★ Lavender
★ A bowl of water

THE SPELL

1. Light the candle.
2. Sprinkle the lavender into your bowl of water.
3. Place your fingers into the lavender-infused water.
4. Close your eyes and feel the healing energy of water moving through you.
5. Envision yourself diving into a beautiful lake.
6. Recite:

   "I call on the element of water to banish my fear of water and fear of swimming. So may it be."

7. Flush your bowl of lavender water down the toilet.
8. Blow out the candle

DREAM RECALL

Dreams are powerful messages from your deep unconscious. We have many dreams each night, but it can be challenging to remember them! This charm bag will help you recall your nightly dreams.

You will need:

★ Herbs: rosemary and mugwort
★ A small pouch

THE SPELL

1. Add the herbs to your pouch.
2. Close the pouch and hold it in your hands.
3. Close your eyes and envision yourself waking up and remembering your dreams.
4. Recite:
   "I call on the element of water to remember my dreams. So may it be."
5. Place your charm bag under your pillow.

PSYCHIC DREAMING

Dreams are amazing opportunities to receive downloads and insights. In psychic dreaming, you dream of an event before it occurs. Here is a spell to help activate or deepen your psychic dreaming abilities.

You will need:

★ A candle
★ A crystal: amethyst

THE SPELL

1. Light the candle.
2. Hold the crystal in your hand.
3. Relax into your mediation and feel the warmth and energy behind your closed eyes.
4. Envision yourself and the crystal being filled with powerful energy.
5. Visualize your third eye being opened.
6. Move your crystal in circular motions in front of your third eye.
7. Recite:
   "Through the power of the element of water, I activate psychic dreaming. So may it be."
8. Place the crystal under your pillow.
9. Blow out the candle.

DREAM ACTIVATOR

Dreams are nightly messages from our unconscious mind, brimming with valuable insights and guidance, often helpful for spiritual work. If you want to have more frequent dreams, try this dream activator spell.

▽

You will need:

★ A candle
★ Herbs: mugwort, rosemary, lavender
★ A bowl of water
★ A pen and paper

THE SPELL

1. Light the candle.
2. Sprinkle the herbs into the bowl of water and stir.
3. On a piece of paper, write the words: "I activate my dreams".
4. Fold the paper and mark it with the symbol for water.
5. Close your eyes and feel the healing energy of water moving through you.
6. Recite:
   "I call on the element of water to activate my dreams. So may it be."
7. Place your folded paper on your altar, with your bowl of herb-infused water on top.
8. Blow out the candle.
9. Let your potion stay on your altar for seven nights and then dispose of it.

DREAM INCUBATION

A lot can be achieved as you move into the realm of dreams. You can set intentions to travel to a specific place or meet a specific person. Dream incubation helps to sow the seeds of an idea that can be more deeply explored while dreaming. Here is a dream sigil spell to do before sleep, to invite such visions, and thereby bring more creative inspiration into your waking life.

You will need:

★ A candle

★ A pen and paper

THE SPELL

1. Light the candle.
2. Prepare your sigil: choose a word, or string of words, relating to the object you want to manifest. Drop the vowels and any duplicate letters. So, for example, if you are using the word: "rose", you'd use the letters: "R S". Write these letters on your piece of paper, arranging them in a creative way, and add the symbol for water.
3. Hold your sigil.
4. Close your eyes and envision what you want to manifest in your dream.
5. Recite:

   "I call on the element of water to bring [name it here] into my dreams. So may it be."
6. Place your sigil under your pillow.
7. Blow out the candle.

LUCID DREAMING

As you move more deeply into your realms of dreaming you will reach a point where you are ready to lucid dream. A lucid dream is the type of dream where you become fully conscious while dreaming. In other words, you become aware that you are dreaming! This can be very powerful: you can speak to dream guides, fly and have spiritual experiences. Here is a lucid dreaming spell and potion to drink before bed.

▽

You will need:

★ A candle
★ Herbs: mugwort, rosemary
★ A cup
★ Boiling water
★ A strainer

THE SPELL

1. Light the candle.
2. Add the herbs to a cup along with some boiling water.
3. Strain the mixture to remove the herbs.
4. Close your eyes and feel the warmth of the dream brew in your hand.
5. Drink the brew as you feel the healing energy of water moving through you and envision yourself flying in a lucid dream.
6. Recite:
   "I call on the element of water to activate lucid dreaming. So may it be."
7. Blow out the candle.
8. Repeat this ritual for five nights.

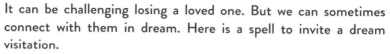

AFTERLIFE VISITATION DREAM

It can be challenging losing a loved one. But we can sometimes connect with them in dream. Here is a spell to invite a dream visitation.

You will need:

★ A candle
★ Your phone

THE SPELL

1. Light the candle.
2. Find a photo of your loved one on your phone.
3. Close your eyes and envision your loved one in your mind's eye.
4. Feel the love and healing energy of your connection to them.
5. Visualize hugging them.
6. Recite:

   "I call on the element of water to connect me to [name the person] in my dreams. So may it be."

7. Send yourself the photo of your loved one with the heart emoji.
8. Blow out the candle.
9. For the next seven nights, gaze upon the photo of your loved one and recite:
   "I call on the element of water to connect me to [name the person] in my dreams. So may it be."

INVITE WORLD PEACE

Not all spells are for ourselves! You may wish to hold good intentions for others, or for our environment. Here is a spell for world peace.

▽

You will need:
★ Your phone

THE SPELL

1. Search for an image of planet earth on your phone.
2. Close your eyes and focus your awareness on the image.
3. Feel love, compassion and peace.
4. Recite:
   "I call on the element of water to bring world peace. So may it be."
5. Send yourself the image with the words: "May there be peace".

FIND YOUR SOULMATE

Your soulmate is out there somewhere, waiting to connect with you. This spell will help to bring them to you.

 ▽

You will need:
★ A candle
★ A Tarot card: the Lovers
★ Rose petals

THE SPELL

1. Light the candle.
2. Place the Lovers card on your altar and sprinkle rose petals around it.
3. Close your eyes and envision yourself as one of the lovers on the card.

4. Visualize yourself embracing your soulmate.
5. Recite:

   "I call on the element of water to connect me to my soulmate. So may it be."
6. Blow out the candle.
7. Leave the Lovers card and rose petals on your altar for two days.

PROTECTION IN SLEEP PARALYSIS

Sleep paralysis is where the body is paralysed but dreaming carries on. Here is a charm to keep with you as you sleep to lessen the fear!

You will need:

★ A candle
★ A crystal: black obsidian
★ Herbs: mugwort and rosemary
★ A small pouch

THE SPELL

1. Light the candle.
2. Put the crystal and herbs in the small pouch.
3. Close the pouch and hold it in your hands.
4. Close your eyes and focus your awareness on the experience of sleep paralysis.
5. Picture yourself blasting light outward, protecting you from the experience.
6. Recite:

   "I call on the element of water to protect me from sleep paralysis. So may it be."
7. Blow out the candle.
8. Place your charm bag under your pillow for 30 days.

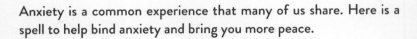

ANXIETY BUSTER

Anxiety is a common experience that many of us share. Here is a spell to help bind anxiety and bring you more peace.

▽

You will need:

★ A candle
★ A Tarot card: the Nine of Swords
★ Lavender
★ Your phone

THE SPELL

1. Light the candle.
2. Place the Nine of Swords card on your altar and sprinkle lavender around it.
3. Close your eyes and visualize the card.
4. Envision yourself as the character on the card. Witness as the scene transforms into something more positive.
5. Picture the blackness on the card turning to light.
6. Recite:
   "I call on the element of water to wash away my anxiety. So may it be."
7. Send yourself an image of the card and lavender on your altar with the words: "I am free of this".
8. Blow out the candle.

RELEASING SADNESS

Sadness or grief can be overwhelming. Especially when it's so close to the surface in our day-to-day lives. In times of need, turn to the power of the moon for magical help. Grief never entirely goes away; we grow around it. Here is a spell to help you find closure and peace.

You will need:

★ The moon
★ A crystal: black obsidian
★ A bowl of water
★ Salt

THE SPELL

1. Focus your awareness on the moon.
2. Close your eyes and feel its light and energy.
3. Recite:
    "I am here. I am alive. Thank you, moon."
4. Place the crystal into the bowl of water. Then dip your fingers in the water, too.
5. Close your eyes again and feel the healing energy of water moving through you.
6. Envision your sadness moving through your fingers into the bowl of water.
7. Recite:
    "I call on the element of water to pull away the sadness within me. So may it be."
8. Remove the crystal from the bowl of water, place it on your altar and sprinkle it with salt.
9. Flush the water down the toilet.

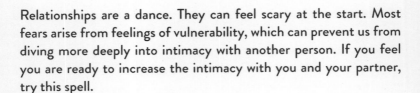

INVITE INTIMACY

Relationships are a dance. They can feel scary at the start. Most fears arise from feelings of vulnerability, which can prevent us from diving more deeply into intimacy with another person. If you feel you are ready to increase the intimacy with you and your partner, try this spell.

You will need:

★ A candle
★ A bowl of water
★ A pen and paper
★ A crystal: rose quartz
★ Rose petals

THE SPELL

1. Light the candle.
2. Place the bowl of water before you.
3. Prepare your sigil: write your initials and your partner's on your piece of paper, arranging them in a creative way, and add the symbols for love and water.
4. Hold your sigil, close your eyes and envision your lover.
5. Visualize yourself filled with love energy and let that love grow within you.
6. Recite:
   "I call on the element of water to deepen the intimacy between [lover's name] and I. So may it be."
7. Place your sigil in the bowl of water. Put the crystal on top of it.
8. Sprinkle rose petals into the bowl of water.
9. Blow out the candle.
10. Leave this on your altar for seven days.

 WATER SPELLS

INCREASE EMPATHY

Empathy is a superpower. It's the ability to sense the emotions and energy of another person. This can be very beneficial when you are working toward becoming a healer or if you live a life of service. This charm jar spell connects us with our empathy, or can boost empathy for those wishing to increase it.

You will need:

★ A candle
★ A jar
★ Herbs: basil and St. John's Wort
★ Rosewater

THE SPELL

1. Light the candle.
2. Prepare your charm jar by adding the herbs and one cup of rosewater.
3. Put a lid on the jar and shake it.
4. Holding the jar in your hand, close your eyes and focus your awareness on your heart.
5. Envision the healing energy of water moving through your heart.
6. Feel love and empathy toward yourself and others.
7. Visualize the loving energy moving into your spell jar.
8. Recite:
   "I call on the element of water to increase my empathy. So may it be."
9. Place your spell jar on your altar.
10. Blow out your candle.

WATER DIVINATION

Divination is the ancient art of receiving information, insights or downloads from non-ordinary states of consciousness. It can be achieved through external tools like mirrors, Tarot cards and even water. This simple water divination spell will bring you messages and guidance. This spell is perfect to use on a full moon.

▽

You will need:

★ A candle

★ A crystal: amethyst

★ A bowl of water

THE SPELL

1. Light the candle.

2. Place the bowl of water before you.

3. Hold your crystal.

4. Close your eyes and feel the healing energy of water moving through you.

5. Envision the water moving through your third eye, and opening it.

6. Recite:

   "I call on the element of water to activate water divination. So may it be."

7. Gaze into your bowl of water and look at the water's reflective surface.

8. Allow yourself to relax and go into a trance-like state, observing any arising thoughts, ideas or images. Stay here for as long as you need to.

9. Blow out the candle.

WATER CRYSTAL CLEANSING

Crystals get a lot of wear and tear and they can only take so much! Crystal cleansing is a good habit to get into if you use these magical stones on a regular basis. Here is a cleansing spell to remove negative energy from your crystals and get them back into optimum working order.

▽

You will need:

★ A candle
★ A bowl of water
★ Salt
★ Your crystal
★ The moon

THE SPELL

1. Light the candle.
2. Place the bowl of water before you and add salt and your crystal.
3. Close your eyes and feel the warmth moving within you.
4. Recite:
   "I call on the element of water to cleanse my crystal of negative energy. So may it be."
5. Blow out the candle.
6. Place the bowl in the moonlight and leave it there overnight.

BALANCE EMOTIONS

Emotions can be a roller-coaster ride in life. Up and down and all around, sometimes they can take over and leave us feeling unbalanced. Here is a water spell that can help bring more balance into your emotional life.

You will need:

★ A candle
★ A bowl of water
★ Ashwagandha
★ Two glasses

THE SPELL

1. Light the candle.
2. Place the bowl of water before you.
3. Add ashwagandha powder to the bowl of water and mix it in.
4. Close your eyes and draw awareness to your imbalanced emotions.
5. Dip your fingers into the bowl of water and envision your negative emotions moving through your fingertips into the water.
6. Recite:
   "I call on the element of water to balance my emotions. So may it be."
7. Pour the bowl of water equally into the two glasses.
8. Place one glass to the right of your altar and one to the left.
9. Blow out the candle.
10. Leave the glasses on your altar for two days and then flush the water down the toilet.

FORGIVE YOURSELF

No one is perfect. There are moments when we mess up and either hurt ourselves and others. It can be difficult to move on and forgive ourselves. Here is a spell to get the ball rolling on some self-compassion and forgiveness.

You will need:

- ★ A candle
- ★ Basil
- ★ A bowl of water
- ★ A towel

THE SPELL

1. Light the candle.
2. Sprinkle the basil into the bowl of water.
3. Close your eyes, focus your awareness on the issue at hand. Make sure you honour your emotions.
4. Envision yourself connecting to the healing energy of water.
5. Picture the water washing away your feelings of guilt.
6. Recite:

   "I call on the element of water to wash away my guilt and initiate forgiveness. So may it be."
7. Bring the water up to your face and cleanse.
8. Do this three times.
9. Dry your face off with a towel.
10. Blow out the candle.

EASING HEARTBREAK

Heartbreak and loss are part of the human experience. Sometimes we find ourselves navigating heartbreak due to a relationship breakup. Here is a spell jar and Tarot magic to help ease a broken heart.

You will need:

★ A candle
★ A Tarot card: the Three of Swords
★ Herbs: hawthorn, basil, motherwort
★ 1 cup rosewater
★ A jar
★ Crystals: lepidolite, rose quartz, rhodonite

THE SPELL

1. Light the candle.
2. Place the Three of Swords card on your altar.
3. Add the herbs and one cup of rosewater to the jar.
4. Put a lid on the jar and shake.
5. Hold the jar in your hand.
6. Close your eyes and focus your awareness on the image of the Three of Swords.
7. Envision the image on the card is your own heart and feel the grief within your heart.
8. Envision the swords falling out of the heart, the heart healing and the clouds moving away.
9. Recite:
   "I call on the element of water to ease my heartbreak. So may it be."
10. Blow out the candle.
11. Place your spell jar on your altar in front of the Three of Swords card. Put the crystals on top of the jar and leave it like this for as long as your grief needs.

BANISH LONELINESS

We all have lonely days where we feel isolated and disconnected. This Tarot spell will help to banish loneliness and invite connectivity.

▽

You will need:

★ A candle
★ A Tarot card: the Hermit
★ A ribbon
★ Your phone

THE SPELL

1. Light the candle.
2. Place the Hermit card in reversed position. Wrap a ribbon around the card and tie it.
3. Close your eyes and focus your awareness on the power of the Hermit card.
4. Envision yourself as the hermit in isolation.
5. Visualize the healing energy of water moving in and carrying the hermit to a place of connectivity.
6. Recite:
   "I call on the element of water to banish my loneliness. So may it be."
7. Send yourself an image of the Hermit card with the words: "I am connected".
8. Blow out the candle.

HEALING FROM BREAKUP

Healing from a breakup can be a lengthy process, and this is normal. Here is a sigil spell jar to help you through the journey toward rediscovering wholeness.

You will need:

★ A candle
★ A pen and paper
★ A jar
★ Basil
★ 1 cup rosewater

THE SPELL

1. Light the candle.
2. Prepare your sigil: write your initials and your ex's on a piece of paper, arranging them in a creative way, and add the symbols for water.
3. Prepare your spell jar by adding the sigil, basil and one cup of rosewater.
4. Put a lid on the jar and shake.
5. Close your eyes and focus your awareness on healing your heart.
6. Envision water energy moving through you.
7. Recite:

   "I call on the element of water to heal me from this breakup. So may it be."

8. Blow out the candle.
9. Place your sigil spell jar on your altar. Leave it there for as long as you need to heal.

CONNECT WITH YOUR
DOLPHIN GUIDE

Dolphins are powerful water elemental guides and harbingers of joy, humour, playfulness, protection and guidance. When called into our lives, dolphin guides bring great magical change and healing. Here is a spell to help you connect to your dolphin guide.

You will need:

★ A candle
★ A bowl of water
★ Your phone
★ Seaweed

THE SPELL

1. Light the candle.
2. Place the bowl of water on your altar.
3. Search for an image of a dolphin on your phone.
4. Close your eyes and focus your awareness on the image of the dolphin.
5. Feel the warmth and positivity of connecting to the dolphin guide.
6. Place the seaweed in the bowl of water and mix.
7. Recite:
   "I call on the element of water to bring connection with my dolphin guide. So may it be."
8. Sit in quiet meditation.
9. Send yourself the image of the dolphin with the words: "My guide".
10. Blow out the candle.
11. Leave the bowl of water and seaweed on your altar for two days.

CONNECT WITH YOUR
MERMAID GUIDE

Mermaids are water elementals and guardians of the watery realms, responsible for bringing emotional healing to those who have experienced trauma. When called into our lives, mermaid guides bring great magical change and healing. Here is a spell to help you connect to your mermaid guide.

▽

You will need:

★ A candle
★ A bowl of water
★ Your phone
★ Seaweed

THE SPELL

1. Light the candle.
2. Place the bowl of water on your altar.
3. Search for an image of a mermaid on your phone.
4. Close your eyes and focus your awareness on the image of the mermaid.
5. Feel the warmth and positivity of connecting to the mermaid guide.
6. Place the seaweed in the bowl and mix.
7. Recite:
   "I call on the element of water to bring connection with my mermaid guide. So may it be."
8. Sit in quiet meditation.
9. Send yourself the image of the mermaid with the words: "My guide".
10. Blow out the candle.
11. Leave the bowl of water and seaweed on your altar for two days.

CONNECT WITH YOUR
UNDINE GUIDE

Undines are water elemental beings and bestowers of harmony with nature, empathy and telepathy. When called into our lives, undine guides bring great magical change and healing. Here is a spell to help you connect to your undine guide.

You will need:

★ A candle
★ Bowl of water
★ Your phone
★ Seaweed

THE SPELL

1. Light the candle.
2. Place the bowl of water on your altar.
3. Search for an image of an undine on your phone.
4. Close your eyes and focus your awareness on the image of the undine.
5. Feel the warmth and positivity of connecting to the undine guide.
6. Place the seaweed in the bowl of water and mix.
7. Recite:

   "I call on the element of water to bring connection with my undine guide. So may it be."

8. Sit in quiet meditation.
9. Send yourself the image of the undine with the words: "My guide".
10. Blow out the candle.
11. Leave the bowl of water and seaweed on your altar for two days.

CONNECT WITH YOUR WHALE GUIDE

Whales are powerful water elemental guides responsible for wisdom, communication, music, healing and psychic abilities. When called into our lives, whale guides bring great magical change and healing. Here is a spell to help you connect to your whale guide.

▽

You will need:

★ A candle
★ Bowl of water
★ Your phone
★ Seaweed

THE SPELL

1. Light the candle.
2. Place the bowl of water on your altar.
3. Search for an image of a whale on your phone.
4. Close your eyes and focus your awareness on the image of the whale.
5. Feel the warmth and positivity of connecting to the whale guide.
6. Place the seaweed in the bowl of water and mix.
7. Recite:
   "I call on the element of water to bring connection with my whale guide. So may it be."
8. Sit in quiet meditation.
9. Send yourself the image of the whale with the words: "My guide".
10. Blow out the candle.
11. Leave the bowl of water and seaweed on your altar for two days.

⊛ SOCIAL MEDIA BOOST

Much of our daily lives is now spent on the internet. Social media is a place where many of us forge livelihoods and careers. It takes a lot of creative brainpower to come up with ideas for posts and videos. Original and engaging content is a skill! Here is a tech spell to boost your creative posting power!

▽

You will need:

★ Your phone

THE SPELL

1. Go to your social media platform and find a post.
2. Under the post, leave a star emoji in the comments and take a screenshot.
3. Close your eyes and focus your awareness on your social media platform.
4. Envision a stream of posts quickly coming into being.
5. Recite:
   "I call on the element of water to activate creative social media posts. So may it be."
6. Send yourself the screenshot with the word: "Activate".

RELEASE ANXIOUS ATTACHMENT

Relationships are hard. Even when in a secure and loving relationship, we can find ourselves becoming anxiously attached. This spell will help to ease the anxiety and bring peace, health and freedom to your relationship.

You will need:

★ A candle
★ A bowl of water
★ Lavender
★ Crystals: obsidian, aquamarine, turquoise, malachite, chrysoprase, kyanite

THE SPELL

1. Light the candle.
2. Place the bowl of water in front of you.
3. Sprinkle the lavender into the bowl of water and mix.
4. Hold the crystal(s) in your hands or create a grid in front of the bowl.
5. Relax into your meditation and feel the warmth and healing energy.
6. Envision yourself and the crystals being filled with powerful healing.
7. Recite:
   "Through the power of the element of water I release anxious attachment to [name the person] and I step into freedom. So may it be."
8. Blow out the candle.
9. Leave the bowl of lavender water and crystal grid on your altar for as long as needed.

CUP HALF-FULL

Perspective is powerful. When we shift our perspective away from feelings of lack, we can clearly see the abundance all around us. Here is a spell to help you clear the emotional pain of the past and lean into gratitude.

▽

You will need:

- ★ A candle
- ★ A Tarot card: the Five of Cups
- ★ A ribbon
- ★ A half-full glass of water

THE SPELL

1. Light the candle.
2. Place the Five of Cups card on your altar.
3. Close your eyes and focus your awareness on the power of the Five of Cups.
4. Envision yourself as the cloaked character on the card and observe the spilled cups and the full cups.
5. Allow yourself to let go of emotional pain.
6. Recite:

   "I call on the element of water to activate a new perspective. I am full of gratitude. So may it be."

7. Bind the Five of Cups card in ribbon and place it in front of the half-full glass of water.
8. Gaze upon the half-full glass and connect with your gratitude.
9. Blow out the candle.
10. Leave the glass for seven days as a daily gratitude reminder.

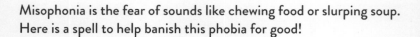

BANISH MISOPHONIA

Misophonia is the fear of sounds like chewing food or slurping soup. Here is a spell to help banish this phobia for good!

▽

You will need:

★ A candle
★ A bowl of water
★ Salt

THE SPELL

1. Light the candle.
2. Place the bowl of water in front of you, add salt and mix.
3. Close your eyes and focus your awareness on your fear.
4. Place your fingers in the bowl and envision the fear moving out of you into the water.
5. Recite:
   "I call on the element of water to banish my misophonia. So may it be."
6. Blow out the candle.
7. Flush the bowl of water down the toilet.

BANISH AGORAPHOBIA

Agoraphobia is the fear of open or crowded spaces. This spell will help you banish the fear once and for all!

▽

You will need:

★ A candle
★ A bowl of water
★ Salt

THE SPELL

1. Light the candle.
2. Place the bowl of water in front of you, add salt and mix.

3. Close your eyes and focus your awareness on your fear.
4. Place your fingers in the bowl and envision the fear moving out of you into the water.
5. Recite:

   "I call on the element of water to release my agoraphobia. So may it be."
6. Blow out the candle.
7. Flush the bowl of water down the toilet.

✳ ACTIVATE YOUR INNER HEALER ✳

Are you feeling called to become a healer? This Tarot spell will help you to connect with compassion and ignite your inner healer.

You will need:

★ A Tarot card: the Queen of Cups
★ Your phone

THE SPELL

1. Place the Queen of Cups card in front of you.
2. Close your eyes and focus your awareness on the power of the Queen of Cups.
3. Envision yourself as the Queen of Cups, full of compassion, wisdom and healing energy.
4. Recite:

   "I call on the element of water to activate my inner healer. So may it be."
5. Send yourself an image of the Queen of Cups card with the words: "I am a healer".

EXPAND YOUR IMAGINATION

Imagination is the beginning of creation. In our daily lives, we often unconsciously rely on imagination to fuel our goals and to articulate our ideas. But sometimes our imagination needs a boost. Here is a crystal spell to expand your imagination to its full potential.

You will need:
- ★ A candle
- ★ A crystal: pyrite

THE SPELL

1. Light the candle.
2. Hold the crystal in your hand.
3. Relax into your meditation and feel the warmth and flowing energy move through you.
4. Envision yourself and the crystal being filled with creative energy.
5. Move your crystal in a circular motion around your head.
6. Recite:
   "Through the power of the element of water I activate my imagination for greater creativity. So may it be."
7. Blow out the candle.

BANISH SELF-SABOTAGE

Self-sabotage is often centred around negative self-talk and self-limiting beliefs. You might feel like you aren't worthy or that you don't deserve nice things. This can impede on your happiness and wellbeing. Here is a spell to help banish this tendency.

You will need:

★ A candle
★ A bowl of water
★ Salt
★ A pen and paper

THE SPELL

1. Light the candle.
2. Place the bowl of water in front of you, add salt and mix.
3. Prepare your sigil: you will be using the word: "Self-sabotage". Drop the vowels and any duplicate letters so you end up with: "S L F B T G". Re-write these letters on your piece of paper, arranging them in a creative way, and add the symbol for water.
4. Fold the paper.
5. Close your eyes and envision the healing energy of water moving through you and washing away your negative beliefs.
6. Recite:
   "I call on the element of water to heal me and banish self-sabotage from my life. So may it be."
7. Place your folded sigil paper in the bowl of water. Submerge it until it's wet.
8. Blow out the candle.
9. Flush the water down the toilet.

BANISH AUTOPHOBIA

Autophobia is the intense fear of being alone. Needless to say, this phobia can be detrimental to life quality. Here is a spell to help banish the fear and bring peace and confidence.

▽

You will need:

★ A candle
★ A bowl of water
★ Salt
★ Small mirror
★ Your phone

THE SPELL

1. Light the candle.
2. Fill the bowl with water, add salt and mix.
3. Hold the small mirror in your hands and gaze at your reflection.
4. Recite aloud the words: "I am not alone".
5. Close your eyes and envision the healing energy of water moving through you, washing over the image of yourself and washing away your fears.
6. Recite:

   "I call on the element of water to banish my autophobia. So may it be."
7. Place the small mirror in the bowl of water.
8. Blow out the candle.
9. Leave it on your altar for as long as needed.

BANISH CLAUSTROPHOBIA

Claustrophobia, the fear of being in a confined space, is something many of us have experienced at one time or other. If it impedes on your ability to feel free, and impacts your wellbeing, this spell is for you.

You will need:

★ Your phone

THE SPELL

1. Search for an image of a confined space you fear on your phone.
2. Close your eyes and focus your awareness on that image of the confined place.
3. Honour the uncomfortable feelings that arise.
4. Visualize the healing energy of water flowing in and washing away the fear.
5. Recite:

   "I call on the element of water to wash away my claustrophobia. So may it be."
6. Send yourself the photo of the confined space with the words: "I am free".

BANISH NECROPHOBIA

Necrophobia is the fear of the dead, and all things associated with death and dying. Death is the great taboo and mysterious unknown. This is why most of us fear it. If the fear of death impedes your happiness and wellbeing, try this Tarot magic spell.

▽

You will need:

★ A candle
★ A jar of water
★ Salt
★ A Tarot card: Death
★ Your phone

THE SPELL

1. Light the candle.
2. Add salt to your jar of water and then put a lid on it.
3. Close your eyes and focus your awareness on the power of the Death card.
4. Envision yourself first as Death riding the pale horse, then as all the other characters on the card.
5. Visualize the healing energy of water washing away your fears.
6. Recite:
   "I call on the element of water to banish my fear of death. So may it be."
7. Send yourself an image of the Death card with the words: "I have no fear".
8. Place the jar of salt water on your altar. Put the Death card on top of the jar.
9. Blow out the candle.

BANISH EROTOPHOBIA

Erotophobia is the fear of sex, sensual and physical intimacy – and it can be a very real thing. Counselling and trauma work may help lessen your phobia's impact on your life, but this empowering and self-loving spell might help, too.

You will need:

★ A bathtub
★ Salt
★ Rose petals
★ Lavender
★ Crystals: black tourmaline, rose quartz
★ Music
★ A candle

THE SPELL

1. Prepare a hot bath. Put the salt, rose petals, lavender and crystals in the water.
2. Play soothing music.
3. Light the candle.
4. Enter the bath.
5. Close your eyes and feel the healing energy of water moving around you.
6. Visualize the water washing away your fears.
7. Recite:
   "I call on the element of water to wash away my fear of sex. So may it be."
8. Stay in your bath for as long as you want.
9. Blow out the candle.

BANISH LOCKIOPHOBIA

The fear of giving birth to a baby is called lockiophobia. Anxiety around labour pains and complications can be present throughout the nine months. Here is a spell to cast to dispel these fears.

▽

You will need:

- ★ A jar
- ★ 1 cup rosewater
- ★ Herbs: raspberry leaf, nettle, lemon balm, fennel
- ★ A pen
- ★ A candle
- ★ Salt

THE SPELL

1. Prepare your spell jar by adding the herbs and one cup of rosewater.
2. Put a lid on the jar and shake.
3. Mark the lid of the jar with the symbol for water.
4. Light the candle.
5. Close your eyes and visualize water energy moving through you.
6. Recite:
   "I call on the element of water to banish my fears. So may it be."
7. Place your spell jar on your altar.
8. Sprinkle a circle of salt around the jar.
9. Blow out the candle.
10. Leave both the jar and circle of salt on your altar for the duration of your pregnancy.

BANISH DENTOPHOBIA

Nobody enjoys a visit to the dentist. For some folks it is so terrifying, they avoid going at all. This becomes a problem when it impacts dental health! Here is a spell to help banish the fear for good.

You will need:

★ Your phone

THE SPELL

1. Search for an image of the perfect smile on your phone.
2. Close your eyes and focus your awareness on that image of the healthy teeth.
3. Observe the thoughts and feelings you have about going to the dentist.
4. Visualize the healing energy of water flowing in and washing away the fear.
5. Recite:
   "I call on the element of water to wash away my fears. So may it be."
6. Send yourself the photo of the healthy smile with the words: "No fear."

BANISH INSOMNIA

Restless nights can cause a lot of stress, especially when you need to get up early for work the next day. Get a good night's sleep with this deep-sleep potion spell.

You will need:

- ★ A candle
- ★ Salt
- ★ A bowl of water
- ★ Herbs: lavender and valerian root
- ★ A cup
- ★ Boiling water
- ★ A tea strainer

THE SPELL

1. Light the candle.
2. Add salt to the bowl of water.
3. Add herbs to a cup along with boiling water.
4. Steep for 20 minutes before straining out the herbs.
5. Close your eyes and focus your awareness on the warm cup of sleep potion in your hands.
6. Drink your tea-potion as you feel the healing energy of water moving through you.
7. Picture yourself having beautiful deep sleep.
8. Recite:

   "I call on the element of water to banish my insomnia. I will sleep deeply tonight. So may it be."

9. Blow out the candle.
10. Place the bowl of salt and water next to your bed for the night.

PMT RELIEF

In the days before your period starts, you might experience an array of unpleasant symptoms, both emotional and physical. Here is a potion spell to keep the PMT away.

▽

You will need:
- ★ A candle
- ★ Salt
- ★ A bowl of water
- ★ Mugwort
- ★ A cup
- ★ Boiling water
- ★ A tea strainer

THE SPELL

1. Light the candle.
2. Add salt to the bowl of water.
3. Add mugwort to a cup along with boiling water.
4. Steep for 20 minutes before straining out the herbs.
5. Place your fingers in the bowl of salt water.
6. Close your eyes and envision your PMT symptoms flowing through your fingers into the bowl of water.
7. Pick up your tea-potion and focus your awareness on the warm cup in your hands.
8. Drink your tea-potion, feeling the healing energy of water moving through you.
9. Recite:
   "I call on the element of water to flush away my PMT. So may it be."
10. Blow out the candle.
11. Take the bowl of salt to the bathroom and flush it down the toilet.

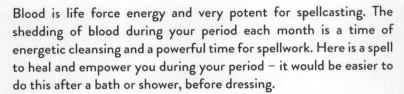

PERIOD POWER

Blood is life force energy and very potent for spellcasting. The shedding of blood during your period each month is a time of energetic cleansing and a powerful time for spellwork. Here is a spell to heal and empower you during your period – it would be easier to do this after a bath or shower, before dressing.

You will need:

★ Menstrual blood
★ A small jar
★ A candle

THE SPELL

1. Collect some of your menstrual blood in a small jar.
2. Light the candle.
3. Hold your jar of blood.
4. Close your eyes and feel the healing energy of water moving through you.
5. With your finger, dab some blood from the jar and mark a blood point on each of your seven chakra points.
6. Recite:

   "I call on the element of water to empower me and my life force energy to activate my chakras. So may it be."

7. Blow out the candle.

MOON MASK BEAUTY

The energetic cleansing initiated by your period can be uncomfortable and a time when you feel less attractive. Here is a spell to enhance your beauty whilst you are on your period.

You will need:

★ Menstrual blood
★ A small jar
★ A candle

THE SPELL

1. Collect some of your menstrual blood in a small jar.
2. Wash your face and remove your makeup.
3. Light the candle.
4. Hold your jar of blood.
5. Close your eyes and feel the healing energy of water moving through your body.
6. With your finger, dab some blood from the jar and apply the blood to your face like a mud mask.
7. Recite:

   "I call on the element of water to activate my beauty and life force energy. So may it be."
8. Keep the mask on your face for 20 minutes and then wash it off.
9. Blow out the candle.

MENOPAUSE RELIEF

Moving into perimenopause and menopause is moving into the wisdom years. Of course, this new chapter of life can bring with it unpleasant symptoms: hot flashes, mood swings and brain fog. Here is a potion spell to help alleviate these symptoms.

You will need:

★ A candle
★ Salt
★ A bowl of water
★ Herbs: red clover, black cohosh, motherwort
★ A cup
★ Boiling water
★ A tea strainer

THE SPELL

1. Light the candle.
2. Add salt to the bowl of water.
3. Add herbs to the cup along with boiling water.
4. Steep for 20 minutes before straining out the herbs.
5. Place your fingers in the bowl of salt water.
6. Close your eyes and envision your menopause symptoms flowing through your fingers into the bowl of water. Give all tensions away to the water.
7. Pick up your tea-potion and focus your awareness on the warm cup in your hands.
8. Drink your tea-potion, feeling the healing energy of water moving through you.
9. Recite:
   "I call on the element of water to flush away my symptoms. So may it be."
10. Take the bowl of salt to the bathroom and flush it down the toilet.
11. Blow out the candle.

STOP MY PERIOD

Ever felt like your period is going on forever? Sometimes we want it to end because of social arrangements or a date. Here is a potion spell to help it stop.

▽

You will need:

★ A candle
★ Salt
★ A bowl of water
★ Herbs: ginger, fennel, raspberry leaf
★ A cup
★ Boiling water
★ A tea strainer

THE SPELL

1. Light the candle.
2. Add salt to the bowl of water.
3. Add herbs to the cup along with boiling water.
4. Steep for 20 minutes before straining out the herbs.
5. Place your fingers in the bowl of salt water.
6. Close your eyes and envision your period flushing away into the bowl.
7. Pick up your tea-potion and focus your awareness on the warm cup in your hands.
8. Drink your tea-potion, feeling the healing energy of water moving through you.
9. Recite:
   "I call on the element of water to stop my period. So may it be."
10. Take the bowl of salt to the bathroom and flush it down the toilet.
11. Blow out the candle.

PERIOD COME QUICK!

Sometimes we want our period to arrive! It could be that it's late or that you want to start sooner so you can finish before an important date in your calendar. Here is a spell potion to welcome your monthly release.

▽

You will need:

★ A candle
★ A pen and paper
★ A bowl of water
★ Herbs: mugwort, parsley
★ A cup
★ Boiling water
★ A tea strainer

THE SPELL

1. Light the candle.
2. Draw the symbol for water on a piece of paper.
3. Fold the paper and put it in your pocket.
4. Add herbs (one or a combination) to the cup along with boiling water.
5. Steep for 20 minutes before straining out the herbs.
6. Pick up your tea-potion and focus your awareness on the warm cup in your hands.
7. Close your eyes and picture starting your period.
8. Drink your tea-potion, feeling the healing energy of water moving through you.
9. Recite:
   "I call on the element of water to activate my period. So may it be."
10. Blow out the candle.

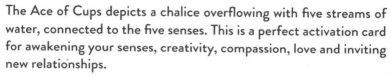

THE ACE OF CUPS

The Ace of Cups depicts a chalice overflowing with five streams of water, connected to the five senses. This is a perfect activation card for awakening your senses, creativity, compassion, love and inviting new relationships.

You will need:

- ★ A Tarot card: the Ace of Cups
- ★ Your phone

THE SPELL

1. Place the Ace of Cups card on your altar.
2. Close your eyes and focus your awareness on the power of the Ace of Cups.
3. Envision yourself as the cup, senses overflowing.
4. Welcome the energy of water and the compassion, creativity and love that spring forth.
5. Recite:
   "I call on the element of water to activate my senses like the Ace of Cups. So may it be."
6. Send yourself an image of the card with the words: "My cup runneth over".

HEALING FROM A TOXIC NARCISSIST

The intensity of being in a relationship with a toxic narcissist can be traumatic. It can take a while to heal from the emotional abuse and gaslighting. Alongside getting the help and care you need, try this spell to help with the process.

▽

You will need:

★ A candle
★ A jar
★ Water
★ Salt
★ Herbs: lavender, rosemary, chamomile, lemon balm, mint
★ A pen
★ A Tarot card: the Devil
★ Your phone

THE SPELL

1. Light the candle.
2. Fill your jar with water, add the salt and herbs, and mix.
3. Put the lid on the jar and mark it with the symbol for water.
4. Study the image on the Devil card.
5. Close your eyes and focus your awareness on the power of the Devil card.
6. Envision yourself as one of the characters freeing yourself from the chains.
7. Visualize the healing energy of water washing away your trauma.
8. Recite:
   "I call on the element of water to heal me from the effects of [name the person]. I am free. So may it be."
9. Send yourself the image of the Devil card with the words: "I am free"
10. Place the jar on your altar. Put the Devil card on top of the jar.
11. Blow out the candle.

QUICK ENERGY PURIFICATION

A hectic day can leave little time for self-care. We might notice stale air or bad vibes around us. These might come from yourself, either from stress or a bad mood! Here is a spell to cleanse energy during stressful times.

▽

You will need:

★ Access to a sink

THE SPELL

1. Turn the tap on in the sink.
2. Put your hands under the stream of water.
3. Close your eyes and feel the healing energy.
4. Focus on the negativity that you want to wash away.
5. Recite:

   "I call in the power of water to wash away this negative energy. I am purified. So may it be."

6. Shake your hands under the water.
7. Turn off the tap.
8. Dry your hands.

SPIRITUAL PURIFICATION BATH

For important magical events, including the new moon, full moon or solstices, it is important to purify yourself. This can be done through a wide variety of methods, such as smoke cleansing and crystals. Here is a sumptuous purification ritual to get you ready for your magical events, to be performed in a bath.

You will need:

★ A bathtub
★ Salt
★ Frankincense oil
★ Lavender
★ Crystals: black tourmaline, rose quartz, amethyst
★ Music
★ A candle

THE SPELL

1. Prepare a hot bath and add the salt, frankincense, lavender and crystals.
2. Play soothing music.
3. Light the candle.
4. Enter the bath.
5. Close your eyes and feel the healing energy of water moving around you.
6. Envision the water washing away energy that is not serving.
7. Recite:
   "I call on the element of water to wash away negative energy and prepare me for [name the ritual]. So may it be."
8. Blow out the candle.

EMPATH CHARM BAG

Empaths are highly intuitive and sensitive people who can sometimes absorb a lot of what other folks are feeling. And although most empaths are healers, they sometimes forget to take care of themselves! Here is a charm bag spell to help balance energy.

You will need:

- ★ A candle
- ★ Crystals: rose quartz, black obsidian
- ★ Rose petals
- ★ Lavender
- ★ A small pouch

THE SPELL

1. Light the candle.
2. Prepare your charm bag by adding the crystals, rose petals and lavender to a small pouch.
3. Close the pouch and hold it in your hands.
4. Close your eyes and visualize healing water energy moving through you and the charm bag.
5. Recite:
   "I call on the element of water to keep me energetically and emotionally balanced. So may it be."
6. Blow out the candle.
7. Place your charm bag in your purse or bag, or keep it under your pillow. Keep it there for 30 nights.

SHOWER POWER

Showers are powerful magical tools for energy purification, empowerment and rebalancing energy. Here is a spell to harness the energy of water in our households, for a powerful energetic reset.

▽

You will need:

★ Access to a shower

THE SPELL

1. Turn on the shower and step in.
2. Close your eyes and feel the healing energy of the water.
3. Focus on the negativity or weakness that you want to wash away.
4. Recite:
   "I call in the power of water to wash away [name the issue]. Empower me with your energy. So may it be."
5. Turn off the shower and exit the shower.

RIVER POWER

For thousands of years, rivers meant life. Humans have congregated around them for fishing, travel, washing and sacred ritual. Here is a simple spell to connect to the sacredness of the river.

▽

You will need:

★ Access to a river (check the currents and dangers first!)

THE SPELL

1. Immerse yourself in the river, either fully or partially. Make sure your hands and feet are touching the water.

2. Close your eyes and feel the healing energy of the water.

3. Recite:

   "I call in the power of water to [say your intention]. Empower me with your energy. So may it be."

4. Exit the river and dry off.

 # LAKE HEALING

Sacred lakes and calming pools have been part of human spiritual traditions for thousands of years. Here is a spell to connect with the sacredness of the lake.

You will need:

★ Access to a lake (lake is safe to swim in!)

THE SPELL

1. Immerse yourself in the lake, either fully or partially. Make sure your hands and feet are touching the water.

2. Close your eyes and feel the healing energy of the water.

3. Recite:

   "I call in the power of water to [say your intention]. Heal me with your energy. So may it be."

4. Exit the lake and dry off.

PUDDLE POWER

Living in cities can mean less access to rivers and lakes. After rainfall we do have access to puddles though! Here is a spell to help you connect to the magic element of water and enhance your intentions.

▽

You will need:
★ A puddle

THE SPELL

1. Touch the puddle with the tip of your foot.
2. Close your eyes and feel the healing energy of the water.
3. Recite:
   "I call in the power of water to [say your intention]. Empower me with your energy. So may it be."
4. Remove contact from the puddle.

RAIN WATER

Rain is a great opportunity to work with the element of water for magical purposes. Here is a spell to help you connect to the magic element of water, on the go, and enhance your intentions. Just to let you know: you will get wet!

▽

You will need:
★ Rain

THE SPELL

1. Step out into the rain.
2. Close your eyes and feel the healing energy of the water.

3. Recite:

   "I call in the power of water to [say your intention]. Empower me with your energy. So may it be."

4. Step out of the rain and dry off.

 # LOVE YOURSELF

For some of us, our default setting can be that we love others more than we love ourselves. It's much easier to give love than to receive it. This can leave us feeling exhausted and sad. Here is a self-love spell to help energize you and activate self-compassion.

You will need:

★ A bathtub
★ Rose petals
★ Lavender
★ Music
★ A candle

THE SPELL

1. Prepare a hot bath and sprinkle the rose petals and lavender into the water.
2. Play soothing music.
3. Light the candle.
4. Enter the bath and close your eyes.
5. Feel the healing energy of water moving around you.
6. Envision yourself diving into a beautiful lake.
7. Recite:

   "I call on the element of water to deepen my self-love. So may it be."

8. Blow out the candle.

THE HIGH PRIESTESS

The High Priestess is the most intuitive archetype in the Tarot deck. A true witchy woman, she has psychic abilities and sits between the veil of both worlds. This simple Tarot spell will help to activate your inner High Priestess and initiate you into your deep witchy abilities.

▽

You will need:

★ A Tarot card: the High Priestess
★ Your phone

THE SPELL

1. Place the High Priestess card on your altar.
2. Close your eyes and focus your awareness on the power of the High Priestess.
3. Envision yourself as the High Priestess, stepping into your power.
4. Recite:
   "I call on the element of water to initiate me as a High Priestess. So may it be."
5. Send yourself an image of the card with the words: "I am a high priestess".

THE KNIGHT OF CUPS

Some chapters in life feel devoid of romance. Everyone loves a bit of romance! It brings joy and fresh energy into our lives. The Knight of Cups is one of the most romantic archetypes in the Tarot deck. The Knight shows up in life to bring more beauty, charm, romantic gestures and love. Here is a spell to draw more romance in your day-to-day.

You will need:

★ A Tarot card: the Knight of Cups

★ Your phone

THE SPELL

1. Place the Knight of Cups card on your altar.
2. Close your eyes and focus your awareness on the power of the Knight of Cups.
3. Envision the energy of the Knight of Cups coming into your life.
4. Recite:

   "I call on the element of water to bring the Knight of Cups energy into my life. So may it be."

5. Send yourself an image of the card with the words: "More romance".

EARTH
SPELLS

Elemental earth magic is perfect for spring, earthing, grounding, burying, banishing, growing, money, materialism, partnerships, relationships, fertility, health, home, plants and animals. In each of the earth spells, it is important to envision the energy of the earth moving through you, contributing its power to your intentions.

NEW MOON IN VIRGO

The new moon holds potent energy for setting an intention to manifest something new. The new moon in Virgo is a perfect time for calling new energies of organization, pragmatism and service into your life.

You will need:

★ A candle
★ A pen and paper
★ A jar
★ Fennel
★ Soil
★ A Tarot card: the Hermit

THE SPELL

1. Light the candle.
2. Focus on your intention and visualize it coming into being.
3. Write your intention on a piece of paper.
4. Fold the paper and mark it with the symbols for the new moon, Virgo and Mercury.
5. Prepare your spell jar by adding the sigil, fennel and soil in the jar.
6. Hold the jar in your hands and close your eyes.
7. Recite:
   "By the power of the new moon in Virgo and the element of earth I manifest my intention. So may it be."
8. Place your spell jar on your altar, with the Hermit card on top.
9. Blow out the candle.

NEW MOON IN CAPRICORN

The new moon holds potent energy for setting an intention to manifest something new. The new moon in Capricorn is a perfect time for calling new energies of enterprise, ambition and productivity into your life.

You will need:

- ★ A candle
- ★ A pen and paper
- ★ A jar
- ★ Tarragon
- ★ Soil
- ★ A Tarot card: the Devil

THE SPELL

1. Light the candle.
2. Focus on your intention and visualize it coming into being.
3. Write your intention on a piece of paper.
4. Fold the paper and mark it with the symbols for the new moon, Capricorn and Saturn.
5. Prepare your spell jar by adding the sigil, tarragon and soil.
6. Hold the jar in your hands and close your eyes.
7. Recite:

   "By the power of the new moon in Capricorn and the element of earth I manifest my intention. So may it be."

8. Place your spell jar on your altar. Put the Devil card on top of the jar.
9. Blow out the candle.

NEW MOON IN TAURUS

The new moon holds the most potent energy for setting an intention to manifest something new. The new moon in Taurus is a perfect time for calling new energies of creativity, dedication and pleasure into your life.

You will need:

- ★ A candle
- ★ A pen and paper
- ★ A jar
- ★ Mint
- ★ Soil
- ★ A Tarot card: the Empress

THE SPELL

1. Light the candle.
2. Focus on your intention and visualize it coming into being.
3. Write your intention on a piece of paper.
4. Fold the paper and mark it with the symbols for the new moon, Taurus and Venus.
5. Prepare your spell jar by adding the sigil, mint and soil.
6. Hold the jar in your hands and close your eyes.
7. Recite:

   "By the power of the new moon in Taurus and the element of earth I manifest my intention. So may it be."
8. Place your spell jar on your altar. Put the Empress card on top of the jar.
9. Blow out the candle.

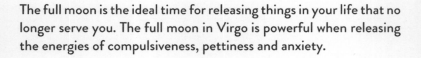

FULL MOON IN VIRGO

The full moon is the ideal time for releasing things in your life that no longer serve you. The full moon in Virgo is powerful when releasing the energies of compulsiveness, pettiness and anxiety.

You will need:

★ A candle
★ A marker
★ A leaf
★ Salt
★ Fennel
★ String
★ Access to the outdoors/soil

THE SPELL

1. Light the candle.
2. Prepare your leaf sigil: you will be using the word: "Release". Drop the vowels and any duplicate letters so you end up with: "R L S". Write these letters on your leaf, arranging them in a creative way, and add the symbols for earth, full moon and Virgo.
3. Sprinkle salt and fennel on the leaf sigil.
4. Roll the leaf and bind it with string.
5. Hold your leaf sigil and envision yourself filled with powerful earth energy.
6. Visualize your energetic release travelling into the leaf.
7. Recite:
   "By the power of the full moon in Virgo and the element of earth I release [name the issue] and I set myself free. So may it be."
8. Go outdoors and dig a hole in the earth. Place your sigil leaf in the hole and cover it up with soil.
9. Blow out the candle.

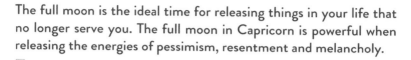

FULL MOON IN CAPRICORN

The full moon is the ideal time for releasing things in your life that no longer serve you. The full moon in Capricorn is powerful when releasing the energies of pessimism, resentment and melancholy.

You will need:

★ A candle
★ A marker
★ A leaf
★ Salt
★ Tarragon
★ String
★ Access to the outdoors/soil

THE SPELL

1. Light the candle.
2. Prepare your leaf sigil: you will be using the word: "Release". Drop the vowels and any duplicate letters so you end up with: "R L S". Write these letters on your leaf, arranging them in a creative way, and add the symbols for earth, full moon and Capricorn.
3. Sprinkle salt and tarragon on the leaf sigil.
4. Roll the leaf and bind it with string.
5. Hold your leaf sigil as you envision yourself and the sigil filled with powerful earth energy.
6. Visualize your energetic release travelling into the leaf.
7. Recite:
   "By the power of the full moon in Capricorn and the element of earth I release [name the issue] and I set myself free. So may it be."
8. Go outdoors and dig a hole in the earth. Place your sigil leaf in the hole and cover it up with soil.
9. Blow out the candle.

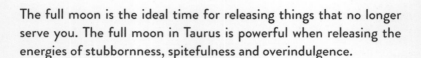

FULL MOON IN TAURUS

The full moon is the ideal time for releasing things that no longer serve you. The full moon in Taurus is powerful when releasing the energies of stubbornness, spitefulness and overindulgence.

You will need:

★ A candle
★ A marker
★ A leaf
★ Salt
★ Mint
★ String
★ Access to the outdoors/soil

THE SPELL

1. Light the candle.
2. Prepare your leaf sigil: you will be using the word: "Release". Drop the vowels and any duplicate letters so you end up with: "R L S". Write these letters on your leaf, arranging them in a creative way, and add the symbols for earth, full moon and Taurus.
3. Sprinkle salt and mint on the leaf sigil.
4. Roll the leaf and bind it with string.
5. Hold your leaf sigil as you envision yourself filled with powerful earth energy.
6. Visualize your energetic release travelling into the leaf.
7. Recite:
   "By the power of the full moon in Taurus and the element of earth I release [name the issue] and I set myself free. So may it be."
8. Go outdoors and dig a hole in the earth.
9. Place your sigil leaf in the hole and cover it up with soil.
10. Blow out the candle.

SOLAR RETURN VIRGO

It's your birthday! Birthdays hold potent energy for spellwork. Time to honour the return of the sun to the natal chart position that you were born in. Use this spell to activate a year ahead of new habits and routines.

You will need:

★ A candle
★ A pen and paper
★ Access to the outdoors/soil
★ Fennel
★ Tarot cards

THE SPELL

1. Light the candle.
2. Close your eyes and connect to your intention.
3. Write your birthday wish on a piece of paper.
4. Fold the paper and mark it with the symbols for the sun, Virgo and Mercury.
5. Close your eyes and envision the energy of earth moving through you.
6. Recite:

   "I honour the sun and my life on this day of my solar return. I call on the element of earth. Move quickly to activate my purpose and manifest my wishes this coming year. So may it be."

7. Go outdoors and dig a hole in the earth.
8. Sprinkle some fennel in the hole.
9. Place your birthday wish paper in the hole and cover it up with soil.
10. Pull a Tarot card for a message for the year ahead.
11. Blow out the candle.

SOLAR RETURN CAPRICORN

It's your birthday! Birthdays hold potent energy for spellwork. Time to honour the return of the sun to the natal chart position that you were born in. Use this spell to activate structure, resilience and success.

You will need:

★ A candle
★ A pen and paper
★ Access to the outdoors/soil
★ Tarragon
★ Tarot cards

THE SPELL

1. Light the candle.
2. Close your eyes and connect to your intention.
3. Write your birthday wish on a piece of paper.
4. Fold the paper and mark it with the symbols for the sun, Capricorn and Saturn.
5. Close your eyes and envision the energy of earth moving through you.
6. Recite:

   "I honour the sun and my life on this day of my solar return. I call on the element of earth. Move quickly to activate my purpose and manifest my wishes this coming year. So may it be."

7. Go outdoors and dig a hole in the earth.
8. Sprinkle some tarragon in the hole.
9. Place your birthday wish paper in the hole and cover it up with soil.
10. Pull a Tarot card for a message for the year ahead.
11. Blow out the candle.

SOLAR RETURN TAURUS

It's your birthday! Birthdays hold potent energy for spellwork. Time to honour the return of the sun in the natal chart position that you were born in. Use this spell to invite a more healthy and vibrant year ahead.

You will need:

★ A candle
★ A pen and paper
★ Access to the outdoors/soil
★ Mint
★ Tarot cards

THE SPELL

1. Light the candle.
2. Close your eyes and connect to your intention.
3. Write your birthday wish on a piece of paper.
4. Fold the paper and mark it with the symbols for the sun, Taurus and Venus.
5. Close your eyes and envision the energy of earth moving through you.
6. Recite:
   "I honour the sun and my life on this day of my solar return. I call on the element of earth. Move quickly to activate my purpose and manifest my wishes this coming year. So may it be."
7. Go outdoors and dig a hole in the earth.
8. Sprinkle some mint in the hole.
9. Place your birthday wish paper in the hole and cover it up with soil.
10. Pull a Tarot card for a message for the year ahead.
11. Blow out the candle.

WINTER SOLSTICE

Winter is coming! Known for being the shortest day, midwinter occurs on December 21 or 22 in the Northern Hemisphere. This celestial event is symbolically linked to the death and rebirth of the sun. Try this spell to connect with solstice energies, potent for stepping out of old ways and inviting in new versions of ourselves.

You will need:

★ A candle
★ A charcoal disc
★ A cauldron
★ Resin: frankincense
★ A pen and paper
★ Salt
★ Herbs: cedar, cinnamon, clove, hawthorn, mistletoe, pine
★ Offerings: orange, cinnamon sticks, evergreen branches
★ A jar
★ Access to the outdoor/soil

Preparation:

★ Grind the herbs into a herbal blend.

THE SPELL

1. Light the candle.
2. Light the charcoal disc and place it in your cauldron.
3. Sprinkle frankincense on the hot coal.
4. Write your intention on a piece of paper.
5. Fold the paper and mark it with the symbol for the sun.
6. Put the sigil, salt, herbal blend and offerings in the jar. Put the lid on the spell jar.
7. Hold the jar in your hands and close your eyes. Envision the energy of earth moving through you.
8. Recite:
   "I call on the element of earth and the life-giving energy of the sun. Release me from the things that no longer serve me."
9. Go outdoors and dig a hole in the earth. Place your spell jar in the hole and cover it up with soil.
10. Blow out the candle.

EARTH SPELLS

IMBOLC

Imbolc marks the beginning of spring and is usually celebrated on 1 February in the Northern Hemisphere. (1 August in the Southern Hemisphere.) The date marks the astronomical midpoint between the winter solstice and spring equinox. Try casting this spell to clear out the old and make way for the new.

You will need:

- ★ A candle
- ★ A bowl of soil
- ★ Salt
- ★ Herbs: angelica, basil, chamomile, heather
- ★ A crystal: clear quartz

THE SPELL

1. Light the candle.
2. Place the bowl of soil in front of you.
3. Close your eyes and envision the old energy that you want to cast away.
4. Place your hands in the bowl of soil and visualize your old energy moving into the soil.
5. Recite:

   "I call on the element of earth to clear out the old and welcome the new. So may it be."
6. Add the salt, herbs and crystal to the bowl.
7. Blow out the candle.
8. Place the bowl on your altar overnight.
9. The next morning, return the soil to the earth.

FERTILITY ACTIVATOR

Having a child is a highlight in many people's lives, but some of us struggle to conceive. Here is a fertility spell to increase your chances.

You will need:

★ A candle
★ A white rose
★ Access to the outdoors/soil
★ Herbs: black cohosh, ashwagandha, chasteberry, shatavari

THE SPELL

1. Light the candle.
2. Hold the white rose in your hands.
3. Close your eyes and envision the nurturing earth energy moving through you.
4. Connect to your intentions for conceiving.
5. Visualize fertile energy moving through you and the rose.
6. Envision your baby.
7. Recite:
   "I call on the element of earth to make me fertile and activate conception. So may it be."
8. Go outdoors and dig a hole in the earth.
9. Pluck the rose petals and place them in the hole along with the herbal blend.
10. Cover it up with soil.
11. Blow out the candle.

MONEY ACTIVATOR

It's no fun being broke or in between paychecks. Invite more money into your life with this quick spell.

You will need:

★ A candle
★ A coin
★ A shoe

THE SPELL

1. Light the candle.
2. Hold the coin in your hand.
3. Close your eyes and envision the abundant earth energy moving through you.
4. Connect to your intentions for receiving money.
5. Visualize your coin multiplying into thousands of coins.
6. Recite:
   "I call on the element of earth to bring me money. So may it be."
7. Place the coin in your shoe and keep it on your altar for seven days.
8. Blow out the candle.

RECEIVE A MORTGAGE

You are on the verge of finding your dream home, but you need a mortgage first. The red tape can feel daunting. Here is a spell to help the mortgage go through and bring in your new home.

You will need:

★ A candle
★ Your phone
★ A coin

THE SPELL

1. Light the candle.
2. Search for an image of the house you want to buy on your phone.
3. Close your eyes and visualize the abundant earth energy moving through you.
4. Connect to your intentions for the mortgage coming through.
5. Envision yourself in your new home.
6. Recite:

   "I call on the element of earth to receive the mortgage. So may it be."
7. Place your phone on your altar, with the image of your dream house open. Put the coin on top on your phone.
8. Blow out the candle.

EMPLOYMENT PROTECTION

You've finally got the job of your dreams, but you feel nervous about somehow losing it! Cast this spell to hold on to your job.

You will need:

★ A candle
★ A marker
★ A rock

THE SPELL

1. Light the candle.
2. Prepare your rock sigil: you will be using the word: "Protection". Drop the vowels and any duplicate letters so you end up with: "P R T C N". Write these letters on your rock, arranging them in a creative way, and add the symbol for earth.
3. Hold your sigil rock and prepare to meditate.
4. Close your eyes and visualize the grounding earth energy moving through you.
5. Connect to the strength that it brings and envision your job being protected by that strength.
6. Recite:
   "I call on the element of earth to protect my job. So may it be."
7. Place your rock sigil on your altar.
8. Blow out the candle.

JOB INTERVIEW CONFIDENCE

You are on your way to a job interview and naturally feel nervous. Cast this spell to ensure you are your most grounded and confident self, to make your best impression to your prospective employers!

You will need:

★ Access to a tree

THE SPELL

1. Touch the tree.
2. Close your eyes and visualize the grounding earth energy moving through you.
3. Connect to the confidence it brings and envision yourself in your new job.
4. Recite:
   "I call on the element of earth to bring me confidence. So may it be."

NEW JOB BE MINE

Perhaps you're unemployed, or ready to leave your current job and looking for a fresh challenge. Cast this spell to bring in new work!

You will need:

★ A candle
★ A long blade of grass
★ A small pouch
★ A coin

THE SPELL

1. Light the candle.
2. Hold the grass in your hands.
3. Close your eyes and envision the abundant earth energy moving through you.
4. Hold in your mind's eye an image of a new job coming to you.

5. Envision yourself in your new job.
6. Recite:

   "I call on the element of earth to bring me a new job. So may it be."

7. Tie the grass into a knot and place it in the pouch with the coin.
8. Place your charm bag on your altar.
9. Blow out the candle.

NEW CAR BE MINE

Whether you're a first-time car owner, or your old car isn't up to scratch, this spell will help bring a new car your way!

You will need:

★ A candle
★ Your phone
★ Soil

THE SPELL

1. Light the candle.
2. Search for an image of the car you want to buy on your phone.
3. Close your eyes and connect with your desire for a new car.
4. Envision yourself in your new car.
5. Recite:

   "I call on the element of earth to receive my new car. So may it be. "

6. Place the phone with the image of your dream car on your altar. Sprinkle soil around the phone.
7. Blow out the candle.

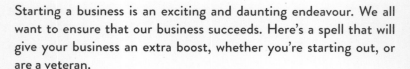

BUSINESS SUCCESS

Starting a business is an exciting and daunting endeavour. We all want to ensure that our business succeeds. Here's a spell that will give your business an extra boost, whether you're starting out, or are a veteran.

You will need:

★ A candle
★ A marker
★ A rock
★ Access to the outdoors/soil
★ Mint
★ Three coins

THE SPELL

1. Light the candle.
2. Prepare your rock sigil: you will be using the word: "Success", and the first letter of your business name. Drop the vowels and any duplicate letters. So, combine the letters "S C" with the first letter from your business name (for Dreamtech, you would add the letter D). Write these letters on your rock, arranging them in a creative way, and add the symbol for earth.
3. Hold your sigil rock.
4. Close your eyes and envision your business becoming a success.
5. Recite:

   "I call on the element of earth to bring success to my business. So may it be."
6. Dig a hole in the soil.
7. Sprinkle some mint in the hole along with the three coins. Place your sigil rock on top of the mint and coins.
8. Cover with soil.
9. Blow out the candle.

NEW ANIMAL COMPANION

Our animal companions are like furry children. They can be a big part of our earthly family, offer us unconditional love, and are also our guides and teachers. Here is a spell to call in your dream animal companion.

You will need:

★ A candle
★ Your phone
★ Basil, rose, yarrow

THE SPELL

1. Light the candle.
2. Search for an image of the animal you wish to adopt on your phone.
3. Close your eyes and connect to your intentions for welcoming in your new companion.
4. Visualize yourself in the company of this animal.
5. Recite:
   "I call on the element of earth to receive my [name the animal]. So may it be."
6. Place the phone with the image of your dream companion on your altar.
7. Sprinkle the herbs around your phone.
8. Blow out the candle.

EARTH SIGIL FOR HEALTH AND HEALING

All of us sometimes feel under the weather. This nurturing spell will support you on the road to recovery.

You will need:

★ Access to the outdoors/soil
★ A stick

THE SPELL

1. Prepare your sigil: you will be using the words "Health healing". Drop the vowels and any duplicate letters, so you end up with: "H L T N G". Combine these with your initials and the symbol for earth.

2. Find a patch of earth and use a stick to etch your sigil into the soil.

3. Close your eyes and envision your health improving.

4. Recite:

   "I call on the element of earth to heal me and bring me good health. So may it be."

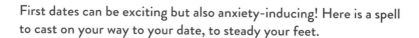

FIRST DATE BLESSING

First dates can be exciting but also anxiety-inducing! Here is a spell to cast on your way to your date, to steady your feet.

You will need:

★ Access to a tree

THE SPELL

1. Touch the tree.
2. Close your eyes and envision your date going well.
3. Recite:

   "I call on the element of earth to bring me confidence for this date. So may it be."

WISH UPON A SQUIRREL

Squirrels are productive creatures. Their appearance reminds us to work hard, preserve and save. They are also symbols of preparation and balance. The next time you see a squirrel, make this wish spell.

You will need:

★ A squirrel

THE SPELL

1. Spot a squirrel.
2. Close your eyes and connect to the inspirational magic of the squirrel.
3. Recite:

   "I call on the element of earth to bring me my wish of [name the wish]. So may it be."

BIND YOUR JUNK FOOD CRAVINGS

We all love a bit of junk food from time to time. But as with all cravings, if it begins to have an adverse effect on your health, it's probably a good idea to rethink our relationship to it! Here is a simple spell to banish those cravings.

You will need:

★ A candle
★ A crystal: amethyst
★ Some candy
★ String
★ A jar
★ Salt
★ Soil

THE SPELL

1. Light the candle.
2. Hold the crystal in your hand.
3. Close your eyes and envision the crystal pulling the cravings out of you, freeing you of them.
4. Recite:
   "I call on the element of earth to bind my junk food cravings. So may it be."
5. Bind the candy with string and place it in the jar.
6. Sprinkle salt and soil into the jar and then add the crystal.
7. Put a lid on the jar and draw the symbol for earth on it.
8. Place the jar on your altar for 30 days.
9. Blow out the candle.

BIND YOUR SMOKING HABIT

Smoking can be a challenging habit to break. We can be at our wits end trying to quit. Here is a spell to help you on your way to a smoke-free life.

You will need:

★ A candle
★ A crystal: amethyst
★ A cigarette
★ String
★ A jar
★ Salt
★ Soil

THE SPELL

1. Light the candle.
2. Hold the crystal in your hand.
3. Close your eyes and envision the crystal pulling the cravings out of you, freeing you of them.
4. Recite:
   "I call on the element of earth to bind my smoking habit. So may it be."
5. Bind the cigarette with string and place it in the jar.
6. Sprinkle salt and soil into the jar and then add the crystal.
7. Put a lid on the jar and draw the symbol for earth on it.
8. Place the jar on your altar for 30 days.
9. Blow out the candle.

BIND YOUR DRINKING HABIT

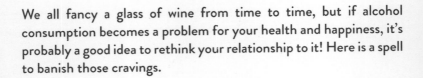

We all fancy a glass of wine from time to time, but if alcohol consumption becomes a problem for your health and happiness, it's probably a good idea to rethink your relationship to it! Here is a spell to banish those cravings.

You will need:

★ A candle
★ A crystal: amethyst
★ A wine cork
★ String
★ A jar
★ Salt
★ Soil

THE SPELL

1. Light the candle.
2. Hold the crystal in your hand.
3. Close your eyes and envision the crystal pulling the cravings out of you, freeing you of them.
4. Recite:
   "I call on the element of earth to bind my drinking habit. So may it be."
5. Bind the wine cork with string and place it in the jar.
6. Sprinkle salt and soil into the jar and then add the crystal.
7. Put a lid on the jar and draw the symbol for earth on it.
8. Place the jar on your altar for 30 days.
9. Blow out the candle.

BANISH MIGRAINE

Nobody likes a migraine! They can be debilitating and reduce our quality of life. Here is a spell to help shift migrainous energy. This spell is most powerful when you're lying outside on the earth.

You will need:

★ A candle
★ A hairbrush
★ Lavender oil
★ Crystals: clear quartz, amethyst
★ A small pouch
★ Herbs: rosemary, mint

THE SPELL

1. Light the candle.
2. Brush your hair as you visualize the energy of the migraine being brushed out.
3. Lie down and anoint your temples with the lavender oil.
4. Place the crystals around your head or on the area where you feel pain.
5. Close your eyes and envision the energy of your migraine being pulled into the earth away from you.
6. Recite:

   "I call on the element of earth to pull the pain of this migraine out of my head. So may it be."
7. After taking as much time as you need in rest, put some of your hair from the brush, the herbs and the crystals in the small pouch.
8. Blow out the candle.
9. Place the pouch under your pillow, or carry around with you until the migraine has subsided.

BANISH TOOTHACHE

Ouch! Toothaches are the worst. You have my sympathies. Here is a quick banishing spell to tide you over before the visit to the dentist.

You will need:

★ A candle
★ A bulb of garlic
★ A cup
★ Some cloves
★ Boiling water
★ Colander
★ A crystal: howlite
★ 2 tbsp salt
★ A toothbrush
★ A ribbon
★ A cotton swab
★ Clove oil

THE SPELL

1. Light the candle.
2. Prepare your potion: finely chop the bulb of garlic and put it in a cup with the cloves and some boiling water. Leave it to steep for 20 minutes. Strain out the garlic and cloves with a colander and put the infused water into a cup with the crystal and salt. Mix the water.
3. Close your eyes and envision the energy of your toothache being pulled into the earth away from you.
4. Bind your toothbrush with ribbon and place it on your altar.
5. Recite:
   "I call on the element of earth to pull away my toothache pain. So may it be."
6. Rinse your mouth for three minutes with the potion. Spit into the sink after rinsing.
7. Soak the cotton swab with multiple drops of clove oil and apply generously to the area of your toothache.
8. Blow out the candle.

BANISH MENSTRUAL PAIN

Period pain can be a monthly nuisance, interrupting daily life. It is however a very potent time for release, magic and spellcasting. If you can get past the pain through this spell you can move forward with some of the other period spells in this book.

You will need:

★ Menstrual blood
★ A small jar
★ A candle
★ Fresh ginger root
★ A teapot
★ Herbs: mugwort, raspberry leaf, cinnamon stick, fennel, chamomile
★ Boiling water
★ A crystal: rose quartz
★ Access to the outdoors/soil

THE SPELL

1. Collect some of your menstrual blood in a small jar.
2. Light the candle.
3. Chop the fresh ginger root and put it in a teapot with the herbs and hot water. Leave it to steep for 20 minutes.
4. Drink your tea-potion.
5. Hold the crystal against your womb.
6. Close your eyes and visualize the energy of your period pain being pulled into the earth away from you.
7. Recite:
   "I call on the element of earth to pull away my period pain. So may it be."
8. Bring your jar of period blood out into the garden (or you can use a pot of soil).
9. Dig a hole and pour your period blood into the hole. Cover it up with soil and mark the spot with the symbol for earth.
10. Blow out the candle.

STRESS RELIEVER

Modern life can be busy. Sometimes we feel as if we've hit our maximum stress levels, and when we ignore it, it starts to wear us down. Here is a grounding spell to help banish the energy of stress.

You will need:

- ★ A candle
- ★ Access to the outdoors/soil
- ★ Sticks
- ★ A crystal: black tourmaline

THE SPELL

1. Light the candle.
2. Draw the symbol for earth in the soil with a stick. Arrange found sticks around the symbol.
3. Hold the crystal in your hands.
4. Close your eyes and envision the energy of your stress being pulled into the earth away from you.
5. Recite:
   "I call on the element of earth to pull away my stress. So may it be."
6. Blow out the candle.

BIND STUBBORNNESS

The rigidity of stubbornness can create blockages that prevent energy from flowing. Our own stubbornness can be the unconscious cause of lack of joy in our lives. Here is a spell to help keep bullheadedness at bay.

You will need:

★ A candle
★ A rock
★ A marker
★ A ribbon
★ Access to the outdoors/soil

THE SPELL

1. Light the candle.
2. Place the rock before you.
3. Prepare your rock sigil: you will be using the word: "Stubborn". Drop the vowels and any duplicate letters so you end up with: "S T B R N". Write these letters on your rock, arranging them in a creative way, and add the symbol for earth.
4. Close your eyes and envision powerful flowing earth energy pushing out your stubbornness.
5. Recite:
   "I call on the element of earth to pull out my stubbornness. I connect with the flow of life. So may it be."
6. Bind your sigil rock with the ribbon.
7. Dig a hole in the earth.
8. Put your sigil rock in the hole and cover it with soil.
9. Blow out the candle.

BANISH THE FEAR OF MONEY LOSS

The fear of losing money can prevent us from allowing its flow – this holds us back from achieving abundance. This Tarot spell will help break the fear and allow money to flow again.

You will need:

★ A candle
★ A Tarot card: the Four of Pentacles
★ A rock
★ A marker
★ A bowl of salt
★ A coin

THE SPELL

1. Light the candle.
2. Place the Four of Pentacles card in front of you.
3. Hold the rock in your hand.
4. Close your eyes and focus your awareness on the power of the card.
5. Envision yourself as the character gripping the coins, then releasing the coins with no fear.
6. Visualize the energy of your fear moving into the rock.
7. In your mind's eye, hold an image of thousands of coins raining down on you.
8. Recite:
   "I call on the element of earth to banish my fear of money. May I be abundant. So may it be."
9. Create your rock sigil by drawing a money symbol on the rock, then add the symbol for earth.
10. Place the bowl of salt on your altar. Put the rock sigil and the coin inside the bowl of salt.
11. Blow out the candle.

HOME RENOVATIONS RUN SMOOTHLY

DIY home renovations are no small task. A team effort is often needed to get things done – you will need to recruit multiple people with multiple skills. Needless to say, chaos can ensue! Here is a Tarot spell to make sure everything runs smoothly.

You will need:

★ A candle
★ A Tarot card: the Three of Pentacles
★ A bowl of salt
★ Mint
★ Rosemary

THE SPELL

1. Light the candle.
2. Place the Three of Pentacles card in front of you.
3. Close your eyes and focus your awareness on the power of the card.
4. Envision yourself as one of the characters, where collaboration and teamwork is running smoothly.
5. Picture your home after the renovations.
6. Recite:
   "I call on the element of earth to make my home renovations run smoothly. So may it be."
7. Put the bowl of salt and herbs on your altar.
8. Place the Tarot card upright in the salt.
9. Blow out the candle.

HOME PROTECTION

Our homes are our sanctuary from the world. We lock our doors to feel safe, ensuring a physical boundary. For additional protection, try this spell.

You will need:

★ A candle
★ A rock
★ A marker
★ Access to the outdoors/soil
★ Salt

THE SPELL

1. Light the candle.
2. Prepare your rock sigil: you will be using the word: "Protection". Drop the vowels and any duplicate letters so you end up with: "P R T C N". Write these letters on your rock, arranging them in a creative way, and add the symbol for earth.
3. Place the rock sigil in front of you.
4. Close your eyes and envision powerful protection energy moving through your rock and all around your house.
5. Recite:
   "I call on the element of earth to protect my house. So may it be."
6. Take your sigil rock outside and dig a hole in the earth.
7. Sprinkle salt into the hole.
8. Put your rock in the hole and cover it with soil.
9. Blow out the candle.

HAPPY HOME

Our households can feel chaotic. In between raising kids and career, there are a lot of energies in the air. This spell is for when household moods are in a slump and need a shift.

You will need:

★ A candle
★ A few long blades of grass – the number should correlate to the number of people living in your house
★ An orange
★ Bowl of salt

THE SPELL

1. Light the candle.
2. Hold the pieces of long grass in front of you.
3. Close your eyes and envision the energy of happiness flowing through you and into the grass.
4. Recite:
   "I call on the element of earth to bring happiness into my home. So may it be."
5. Tie a knot in each blade of grass.
6. Cut a hole in the top of the orange and stick the grass in this hole.
7. Place the orange in the bowl of salt and leave on your altar for seven days.
8. Blow out the candle.

SALT DIVINATION

Divination aided by salt is called alomancy – and it has been performed since ancient times. Salt is a versatile ingredient used in a wide variety of magic, from protection spells through to purification rituals. Try this spell to seek an answer to a question.

You will need:

★ A candle
★ Black cloth
★ A bowl of large sea salt crystals

THE SPELL

1. Light the candle.
2. Place the black cloth in front of you and the bowl of salt crystals next to you.
3. Gather a fist full of salt in your hand.
4. Close your eyes and envision the grounding earth energy moving through you and the salt crystals.
5. Recite:
   "I call on the element of earth to bring me an answer to the question of [name the question]. So may it be."
6. Put the salt crystals on the black cloth.
7. Open your eyes and study the patterns that the salt crystals form on the black cloth. Look for shapes, symbols, numbers, objects or letters. These should bring you closer to an answer to your question.
8. Blow out the candle.

BABY PROTECTION

Being a new mother conjures up all types of instincts, including the maternal drive to protect your offspring. Use this spell to help protect your new baby.

You will need:

★ A candle
★ A pen and paper
★ Soil
★ Salt
★ Rosemary
★ A crystal: lepidolite
★ A jar

THE SPELL

1. Light the candle.
2. Prepare your sigil: write your child's initials on a piece of paper, arranging them in a creative way, and add the symbol for earth.
3. Fold your paper.
4. Put the sigil, soil, salt, rosemary and crystal in your jar. Put the lid on the jar.
5. Hold the spell jar in your hands and close your eyes.
6. Focus your awareness on the earth energy moving through you and the jar.
7. Envision the earth energy surrounding your child, protecting them.
8. Recite:
   "I call on the element of earth to protect my child, [child's name]. So may it be."
9. Place your sigil spell jar on your altar, or in your child's room, for 30 days.
10. Blow out the candle.

BRING BACK A LONG-LOST LOVE

Love never dies. A part of us will always love a person, even if there was a breakup. A long-lost love with whom we've lost touch could feel the same way! Long distance and the passing of time can keep us apart. Here is a spell to bring them back into your sphere, if they feel the same way.

You will need:

★ A candle
★ A rock
★ A marker
★ A magnet

THE SPELL

1. Light the candle.
2. Prepare your rock sigil: you will be using the initials of your long-lost love. Write these letters on your rock, arranging them in a creative way, and add a heart and the symbol earth.
3. Hold the magnet in one hand and your sigil in the other.
4. Close your eyes and envision your long-lost love while connecting the magnet with your sigil.
5. Envision the powerful energy of magnetism drawing your lover back to you.
6. Recite:

   "I call on the element of earth to bring my long-lost love, [name], back to me. So may it be."

7. Place your sigil on your altar. Put the magnet on top.
8. Blow out the candle.

THE ENCHANTED GARDEN

Gardens are amazing places with huge potential for abundance. They are beautiful but can also feed us, nourish and support wildlife, and are teeming with elemental magic. Here is a spell to help bring your garden into its fullest potential for magic and enchantment.

You will need:

- ★ Access to a garden
- ★ A candle
- ★ A mirror
- ★ A wind chime
- ★ Herbs: rosemary, lavender, sage, mint
- ★ A crystal: clear quartz

THE SPELL

1. Go into your garden and lay all the objects in front of you.
2. Light the candle.
3. Close your eyes and envision the powerful energy of magic and enchantment moving through your objects and the garden.
4. Recite:
   "I call on the element of earth to bring magic and enchantment to this garden. So may it be."
5. Take some time to arrange your objects mindfully around the garden: plant the seeds in the soil; assemble the wind chime; place the mirror somewhere among the green and scatter the crystal among the flowers.
6. Blow out the candle.

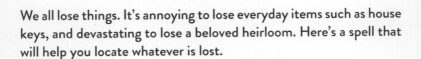

FIND A LOST OBJECT

We all lose things. It's annoying to lose everyday items such as house keys, and devastating to lose a beloved heirloom. Here's a spell that will help you locate whatever is lost.

You will need:

★ A candle
★ A charcoal disc
★ A cauldron
★ Herbs: mugwort, wormwood
★ A crystal pendulum

THE SPELL

1. Light the candle.
2. Light the charcoal disc and place it in your cauldron.
3. Sprinkle the herbs on the hot coal.
4. Hold your pendulum in front of you.
5. Focus your awareness on your heart and allow it to open.
6. Envision the lost object and telepathically call it into your mind.
7. Ask the object where it is.
8. Observe any images coming into your mind.
9. Consult your pendulum for yes or no answers.
10. Recite:
    "I call on the element of earth to locate [name of object]. So may it be."
11. Blow out the candle.

(E) PROTECT YOUR LUGGAGE

The logistics of travelling are quite involved. Between driving to the airport, checking in luggage and rushing to catch flights, there are plenty of opportunities for things to go wrong. Here is a spell to keep your belongings protected before travelling.

You will need:

★ Comfrey
★ A small pouch
★ Your suitcase

THE SPELL

1. Place the comfrey in a small pouch.
2. Place your suitcase in front of you.
3. Close your eyes and envision the powerful energy of protection moving around your suitcase.
4. Recite:
   "I call on the element of earth to protect my luggage. So may it be."
5. Place the bag of comfrey in your suitcase ahead of your journey.

NEW BIRTH CEREMONY

New motherhood is a magical and sacred time for mother and baby. Here is a consecrating spell to help initiate your baby into their life's path and welcome them into the world.

You will need:

★ A candle
★ Some clay
★ A bowl of water

THE SPELL

1. Light the candle.
2. Put the clay in a bowl of water.
3. Close your eyes and envision the powerful energy of protection moving through you both.
4. Recite:
   "I call on the element of earth to bless [baby's name] for their life path. So may it be."
5. Take a small dab of wet clay and anoint your baby's forehead.
6. You can use their astrological symbol or the symbol for earth to represent their arrival in this material reality.
7. Let the clay dry on their forehead.
8. Send blessings to your baby.
9. Blow out the candle.
10. After, gently wash your baby's forehead to remove the clay.

BABY NAMING CEREMONY

Once your baby has arrived, it's time to give them their name. In magical theory, a person's name holds power. Names are important! Here is a beautiful naming ceremony spell to help consecrate your child's name for their journey forward in life.

You will need:

★ A candle
★ A pen and paper
★ A jar
★ Herbs: basil, mugwort
★ Access to the outdoors

THE SPELL

1. Light the candle.
2. Prepare your sigil: you will be using the name of your baby. Drop the vowels and any duplicate letters. So, for example, if your baby's name is Lilly, use the letters: "L Y". Write these letters on your piece of paper, arranging them in a creative way, and add the symbol for earth.
3. Hold the sigil and close your eyes.
4. Envision the grounding earth energy moving through you and your baby.
5. Recite:
   "I call on the element of earth to bless my baby and their name. My baby is named [baby's name]. So may it be."
6. Place the sigil in the jar with the herbs and close the jar.
7. Dig a hole in your garden. Place the jar in the hole and cover it with soil.
8. Send blessings to your baby.
9. Blow out the candle.

PLANT A BABY TREE

After settling into your new routine as a parent, you will notice how quickly your baby grows. Every day brings with it a new change. In honouring the growth of your child along their life path, here is a beautiful planting spell to help honour and grow your child's spiritual life path.

You will need:

★ A candle
★ A charcoal disc
★ A cauldron
★ Resin: frankincense
★ Seeds or seedlings
★ Access to the
  outdoors

THE SPELL

1. Light the candle.
2. Light the charcoal disc and place it in your cauldron.
3. Sprinkle the frankincense onto the hot coal and let the smoke purify the seeds or seedling.
4. Hold the seeds or seedling and close your eyes.
5. Visualize the grounding earth energy moving through you, your baby and the seeds.
6. Recite:
   "I call on the element of earth to bless this seed/seedling of [name the tree] to journey alongside my child's path. This tree is a place for my child to remember their soul journey and to learn and grow. So may it be."
7. Dig a hole in the earth and plant the seed/ seedling. Cover the seed or roots with soil.
8. Send blessings to your baby and the tree.
9. Blow out the candle.

RENEW LOVE

There are times in our relationships where we need a renewal. Especially long-term relationships that fall into routines. Here is a spell to rekindle the love you have with your partner.

You will need:

★ A candle
★ A knife
★ A pomegranate
★ A plate
★ A bowl
★ Flour
★ Basil
★ A white rose

THE SPELL

1. Light the candle.
2. Cut the pomegranate in half and place on a plate.
3. Place the bowl in front of you and add the flour, two halves of the pomegranate and the basil.
4. Hold the white rose and close your eyes.
5. Visualize the grounding earth energy moving through you.
6. Connect to the security that love brings.
7. Envision powerful energy of renewing love moving around you and your partner and into the rose.
8. Recite:
   "I call on the element of earth to renew my love with [partner's name]. So may it be."
9. Pluck the petals from the rose and sprinkle them on the pomegranate.
10. Place the pomegranate on your altar.
11. Blow out the candle.

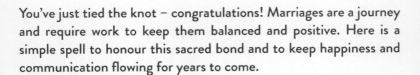

HAPPY MARRIAGE

You've just tied the knot – congratulations! Marriages are a journey and require work to keep them balanced and positive. Here is a simple spell to honour this sacred bond and to keep happiness and communication flowing for years to come.

You will need:

★ A candle
★ Flour
★ Herbs: lavender, oregano, rosemary
★ Crystals: rose quartz, citrine
★ A small pouch

THE SPELL

1. Light the candle.
2. Add the flour, herbs and crystals to your small pouch.
3. Hold the bag in your hands and close your eyes.
4. Visualize grounding earth energy moving through you.
5. Connect to the joy it brings.
6. Envision the powerful energy of positivity and happiness flowing through you and your partner, and channel it into the bag.
7. Recite:
   "I call on the element of earth to maintain happiness and positivity within my marriage to [person's name]. So may it be."
8. Blow out the candle.
9. Place the charm bag in a drawer of your bedside table or dresser and leave it there for 30 days.

RELATIONSHIP PROTECTION

Relationships are beautiful but complex. External factors can sometimes challenge them and cause friction. Here is a sigil spell to help you protect your relationship and bring harmony.

You will need:

★ A candle
★ A rock
★ A marker
★ Access to the outdoors
★ Salt

THE SPELL

1. Light the candle.
2. Prepare your rock sigil: you will be using both your initials and your partner's. Write these letters on your rock, arranging them in a creative way, and add the symbol for earth.
3. Close your eyes and envision powerful protective earth energy moving around you and your partner.
4. Recite:
   "I call on the element of earth to protect my relationship with [person's name]. So may it be."
5. Dig a hole in the earth.
6. Sprinkle salt in the hole.
7. Put your sigil rock in the hole and cover it with soil.
8. Blow out the candle.

RELATIONSHIP CLOSURE

Sadly, some relationships come to an end. You may need closure to move on with your life and begin the healing process. Here is a spell to help initiate this process.

You will need:

★ A candle
★ A rock
★ A marker
★ A pen and paper
★ A cauldron
★ Salt
★ Access to the outdoors

THE SPELL

1. Light the candle.
2. Prepare your rock sigil: you will be using both your initials and your partner's. Write these letters on your rock, arranging them in a creative way, and add the symbol for earth.
3. Hold your sigil rock in your hands and close your eyes. Envision your partner and connect your heart to them.
4. Write a letter to your partner expressing how you feel concerning the end of your relationship.
5. Recite:
   "I call on the element of earth to bring closure to the relationship with [person's name]. So may it be."
6. Fold your letter and light it with the candle.
7. Let the letter burn to ash in your cauldron.
8. Mix the ash with salt to create black salt.
9. Dig a hole in the earth. Sprinkle the black salt into the hole.
10. Place your rock sigil in the hole and cover it with soil.
11. Blow out the candle.

RELEASE RESENTMENT

There are times when resentment creeps into our relationships. Here is a spell to help release this common source of tension and conflict!

You will need:

★ A candle
★ A pen and paper
★ A bowl
★ Salt
★ Crystals: pink opal, rose quartz, amazonite, hiddenite, black obsidian

THE SPELL

1. Light the candle.
2. Prepare your sigil: you will be using the initials of the person you resent. Write these letters on your piece of paper, arranging them in a creative way, and add the symbol for earth.
3. Hold the sigil in your hands and close your eyes.
4. Visualize the grounding earth energy moving through you and pushing out the resentment you have toward this person.
5. Envision healing energy setting you free.
6. Recite:
   "I call on the element of earth to release my resentment toward [person's name]. So may it be."
7. Fold up the sigil. Place the sigil in a bowl and pour salt over it.
8. Put the crystals on top of the salt.
9. Place the bowl on your altar.
10. Blow out the candle.

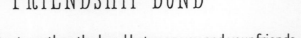

FRIENDSHIP BOND

Here is a spell to strengthen the bond between you and your friends, to help get you through life's ups and downs.

You will need:

★ A candle
★ A long blade of grass
★ A bowl of salt
★ Crystals: black tourmaline, pyrite, smoky quartz, blue lace agate

THE SPELL

1. Light the candle.
2. Hold the long blade of grass in your hands and close your eyes.
3. Envision the energy of strength supporting your friendship.
4. Envision the strength moving into the blade of grass.
5. Recite:
   "I call on the element of earth to strengthen my relationship with [person's name]. So may it be."
6. Tie a knot in the grass.
7. Put the grass in the bowl of salt. Arrange the crystals in a circle around the grass.
8. Place the bowl on your altar.
9. Blow out the candle.

CONNECT WITH YOUR ELF GUIDE

Elves are earth elemental creatures, associated with light, who live in a magical realm as guardians of the forests. When called into our lives, elf guides can act as guardians, healers and teachers. These nature spirits can also help deepen our connection to the natural world and bring more joy into our lives. Here is a spell to cast outside, to connect you with your elf guide.

You will need:

★ Access to the outdoors
★ Some nuts
★ A wooden spoon

THE SPELL

1. Leave an offering of nuts on the ground.
2. Place the wooden spoon next to the offering.
3. Close your eyes and hold the image of an elf in your mind's eye.
4. Feel the warmth and positivity of connecting to the elf guide.
5. Recite:
   "I call on the element of earth to invoke my elf guide. So may it be."
6. Sit in quiet meditation.
7. Write down your impressions or insights in your journal or grimoire.
8. Send out gratitude.

CONNECT WITH YOUR
GNOME GUIDE

Gnomes are earth elemental beings. They are nocturnal and subterranean creatures, and often artisans and smiths. When called into our lives, gnome guides can act as mentors, helping us with anything practical. They can also help us deepen our connection to the natural world and bring more joy into our lives. Here is a spell to cast outside, to help you connect to your gnome guide.

You will need:

★ Access to a forest with a cave or rocky area
★ Some nuts
★ A wooden spoon

THE SPELL

1. Leave the offering of nuts on the ground before you enter the forest.
2. Place the wooden spoon next to the offering.
3. Close your eyes and focus your awareness on an image of a gnome.
4. Feel the warmth and positivity of connecting to the gnome guide.
5. Recite:
   "I call on the element of earth to invoke my gnome guide. So may it be."
6. Sit in quiet meditation.
7. Write down your impressions or insights in your journal or grimoire.
8. Send out gratitude.

CONNECT WITH YOUR ANIMAL GUIDE

Animals have been our guides and teachers since time immemorial. In post-industrial times, however, our connection to animal guides has waned. Here is a spell to get you connected with magical fauna.

You will need:

* ★ A candle
* ★ A pen and paper
* ★ Soil
* ★ Herbs: dandelion, mugwort, elderflower
* ★ A bowl

THE SPELL

1. Light the candle.
2. Close your eyes and focus your awareness on your heart. Allow it to be open and receptive.
3. Recite:
   "I call on the element of earth to bring me my animal guide. So may it be."
4. Sit in quiet meditation.
5. Observe images unfolding in your mind's eye. Which animal appeared to you?
6. Prepare your sigil: you will be using the name of the animal guide from your vision. Drop the vowels and any duplicate letters. So, for example, if you saw a bear, your letters would be: "B R". Write these letters on your piece of paper, arranging them in a creative way, and add the symbol for earth.
7. Put the soil, herbs and sigil in the bowl.
8. Place this bowl on your altar.
9. Blow out the candle.

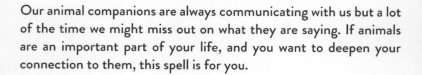

ANIMAL COMPANION PSYCHIC

Our animal companions are always communicating with us but a lot of the time we might miss out on what they are saying. If animals are an important part of your life, and you want to deepen your connection to them, this spell is for you.

You will need:

★ A candle
★ A charcoal disc
★ A cauldron
★ Crystals: serpentine, chrysoprase, kambaba jasper, orthoceras, gem silica, blue tourmaline, lizardite, mokaite
★ Herbs: mugwort, wormwood

THE SPELL

1. Light the candle.
2. Light the charcoal disc and place it in your cauldron.
3. Hold your crystal or create a grid if you have more than one.
4. Sprinkle the herbs on the hot coal.
5. Focus your awareness on your heart and allow it to open.
6. Envision your animal companion or an animal you know.
7. Telepathically say the animal's name in your mind.
8. Ask the animal a question.
9. Observe any images coming into your mind.
10. Connect back to your heart.
11. Recite:

    "I call on the element of earth to activate my psychic communication with animals. So may it be."

12. Blow out the candle.

COMMUNICATE WITH
YOUR PLANTS

The relationship between humans and plants goes back thousands of years. We have relied on plants for nourishment, but also for healing, shelter and magic. Here is a spell to connect with plants to restore mental, physical and spiritual wellbeing.

You will need:

★ A candle
★ A charcoal disc
★ A cauldron
★ Herbs: mugwort, wormwood
★ A crystal: green aventurine
★ A house plant

THE SPELL

1. Light the candle.
2. Light the charcoal disc and place it in your cauldron.
3. Sprinkle the herbs on the hot coal.
4. Place your houseplant in front of you.
5. Hold your crystal.
6. Focus your awareness on your heart and allow it to open.
7. Telepathically connect with your plant and ask it a question.
8. Observe any images coming into your mind.
9. Connect back to your heart.
10. Recite:
    "I call on the element of earth to activate my psychic communication with plants. So may it be."
11. Blow out the candle.

ANIMAL COMPANION PROTECTION

Animal companions are much like family members. Here is a spell to help protect beloved animals.

You will need:

- ★ A candle
- ★ A pen and paper
- ★ Salt
- ★ Rosemary
- ★ Soil
- ★ A crystal: black tourmaline
- ★ A jar

THE SPELL

1. Light the candle.
2. Prepare your sigil: you will be using the initials of your animal companion's name. Drop the vowels and any duplicate letters. So, for example, if the animal's name is Templeton, your letters would be: "T M P L N". Write these letters on your piece of paper, arranging them in a creative way, and add the symbol for earth.
3. Hold your sigil and close your eyes.
4. Envision powerful protective earth energy moving around you and your pet.
5. Recite:
   "I call on the element of earth to protect [pet's name]. So may it be."
6. Put your sigil, the salt, rosemary, soil and crystal in the jar.
7. Put a lid on the jar and seal it with wax from the candle.
8. Blow out the candle.
9. Keep the sigil jar on your altar.

FIND YOUR LOST ANIMAL COMPANION

It is distressing to lose a pet. Local postering and social media posts might help, but try this spell to boost search efforts and have them return safely home. This spell will need to be performed multiple times – during the day, just before bedtime and, if possible, in your dreams.

You will need:

★ A candle
★ 3 tbsp mugwort
★ A teapot
★ Boiling water
★ Crystals: clear quartz, amethyst

THE SPELL

1. Light the candle.
2. Add mugwort to the teapot and fill with boiling water. Leave it to steep for 20 minutes.
3. Hold your crystal(s).
4. Drink your potion as you focus your awareness on your heart.
5. Hold an image of your animal companion in your mind's eye and telepathically call them into your mind.
6. Ask the animal where they are.
7. Observe any images coming into your mind.
8. Connect back to your heart.
9. Recite:
   "I call on the element of earth to locate [pet's name]. So may it be."
10. Blow out the candle.

ENGAGEMENT BLESSING

The love is deepening between you and your partner, and you feel ready to tie the knot. Cast this romantic spell after an engagement to bless it!

You will need:

★ A candle
★ Two long blades of grass
★ A white rose
★ A pen and paper
★ A jar
★ Flour
★ A crystal: rose quartz

THE SPELL

1. Light the candle.
2. Place the two blades of long grass and white rose in front of you.
3. Prepare your sigil: write your initials as well as your partner's on your piece of paper, arranging them in a creative way, and add the symbols for love and earth.
4. Fold your sigil.
5. Hold the blades of long grass, the white rose and your sigil.
6. Close your eyes and envision the energy of love and commitment flowing through you and your lover.
7. Recite:
   "I call on the element of earth to bless the engagement between [partner's name] and I. So may it be."
8. Tie the two pieces of grass in a knot and put them in the jar with the sigil, flour, white rose petals and crystal.
9. Put a lid on the jar and seal it with wax from the candle.
10. Blow out the candle.

HANDFASTING BOUQUET

The coming together of two people is a powerful ritual. Handfasting is a magical ceremony that marks two people's love for one another, and their commitment to walk with each other for life. It's basically a wedding for magical folk! Here is a lovely bouquet spell for your handfasting.

You will need:

★ A candle
★ A charcoal disc
★ A cauldron
★ Flowers: roses, baby's breath, asters, carnations, verbena
★ Herbs: rosemary, dill, lavender
★ White, red and blue ribbons
★ Resin: frankincense

THE SPELL

1. Light the candle.
2. Light the charcoal disc and place it in your cauldron.
3. Cut and prepare the flowers and fresh herbs.
4. Combine the flowers and fresh herbs, arranging them into a bouquet.
5. Use the ribbons to bind the bouquet.
6. Sprinkle some frankincense on the hot coal. Use the smoke to cleanse and bless your bouquet.
7. Hold your bouquet and close your eyes.
8. Envision you and your partner coming together with love, and channel that love into the bouquet.
9. Recite:
   "I call on the element of earth to bless and empower my handfasting. So may it be."
10. Put your bouquet on your altar ready for your big event.
11. Blow out the candle.

HANDFASTING HAIR WREATH

A wreath symbolizes happiness, love, prosperity and a bright future. This spell invites good fortune for the couple.

You will need:

- ★ A candle
- ★ A charcoal disc
- ★ A cauldron
- ★ A measuring tape
- ★ Scissors
- ★ Wire
- ★ Flowers: roses, baby's breath, asters, carnations, verbena
- ★ Herbs: rosemary, dill, lavender
- ★ Florist's tape
- ★ White, blue and red ribbons
- ★ Resin: frankincense

THE SPELL

1. Light the candle.
2. Light the charcoal disc and place it in your cauldron.
3. Measure the circumference of your head. Cut the wire according to this measurement.
4. Fashion the wire into a ring and twist the ends together.
5. Cut and prepare the flowers and fresh herbs.
6. Use the florist's tape to secure the flowers and herbs to the wire ring. Add ribbons as well.
7. Sprinkle some frankincense on the hot coal. Cleanse and bless the wreath with the smoke.
8. Place the hair wreath on your head and close your eyes.
9. Channel your love for your partner into the hair wreath.
10. Recite:
    "I call on the element of earth to bless and empower my handfasting. So may it be."
11. Put your wreath on your altar.
12. Blow out the candle.

WISH UPON A PEBBLE

Rocks and pebbles hold wonderful grounding energy. Next time you are outside and a pebble catches your eye, try this spell to grant a wish.

You will need:

★ A pebble

THE SPELL

1. Find a pebble on the ground.
2. Hold the pebble and close your eyes.
3. Connect to the magic that it brings to you.
4. Set an intention.
5. Recite:

   "I call on the element of earth to manifest [name your wish]. So may it be."

WISH UPON A LEAF

The leaves of the trees are reminders of the impermanence of all things. Here is a spell to cast when a leaf catches your eye – with it you can make a wish for manifesting change.

You will need:

★ A leaf

THE SPELL

1. Find a leaf on the ground.
2. Hold the leaf and close your eyes.
3. Connect to the magic that it brings to you.
4. Set an intention.
5. Recite:

   "I call on the element of earth to manifest [name your wish]. So may it be."

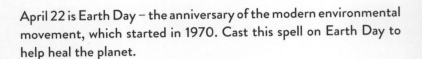 EARTH DAY

April 22 is Earth Day – the anniversary of the modern environmental movement, which started in 1970. Cast this spell on Earth Day to help heal the planet.

You will need:

★ Access to the outdoors

★ A crystal: green aventurine

★ An offering: nuts, seeds, herbs

THE SPELL

1. Sit on the ground and leave your offering.
2. Hold the crystal and close your eyes.
3. Connect to your heart space and love for the planet.
4. Envision green light expanding from your heart outward to the planet.
5. Recite:
   "I connect to the element of earth and to my love of this planet. I send out healing. I send out positive change. So may it be."

WHICH ROAD TO CHOOSE?

Sometimes we find ourselves at life's crossroads and need to make important decisions about which road to journey down. The next time you find yourself at a crossroads on a nature trail, try this spell to conquer indecisiveness!

You will need:

★ A stick, piece of bark or wood

THE SPELL

1. Find a stick or small piece of bark or wood on the ground.

* A crossroad
  on the trail

2. Hold the stick and close your eyes.
3. Connect with the decisions you need
   to make at this crossroad in your life.
4. Recite:
   *"I call on the element of earth to help me make
   the decision for this crossroad in my life. Bring
   synchronicity and answers. So may it be."*
5. Dig a small hole at the crossroad
   and bury the stick.

☼E MUD MAGIC

No one likes to get mud on them. However, mud can help us
magically. Cast this spell to get unstuck in various areas of your life.
▽

You will need:

* Mud
* A stick

THE SPELL

1. Press your foot into the mud
   and close your eyes.
2. Bring into your awareness the area
   in your life where you feel stuck.
3. Envision yourself breaking free.
4. Recite:
   *"I call on the element of earth to release
   me from [name the issue]. So may it be."*
5. Pull your foot away from the mud.
6. Use the stick to draw the symbol
   for earth in the mud.

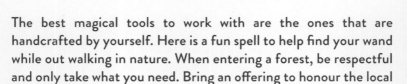

FIND YOUR WAND

The best magical tools to work with are the ones that are handcrafted by yourself. Here is a fun spell to help find your wand while out walking in nature. When entering a forest, be respectful and only take what you need. Bring an offering to honour the local flora and fauna.

You will need:

★ An offering: nuts, seeds, herbs
★ Rosemary

THE SPELL

1. Place your offering for the forest on the ground and sit next to it.
2. Addressing the forest, recite: *"Please guide me to my wand."*
3. Begin your hike, letting your intuition guide you toward a stick.
4. Once you have found your stick, sit back down on the forest floor.
5. Hold the stick in your hand and close your eyes.
6. Recite: *"I call on the element of earth to claim this stick as my wand. Thank you, sacred forest. So may it be."*
7. Bring the wand home and place it on your altar.
8. Burn the rosemary and smoke-cleanse your wand.

EARTH SPELLS

MARK YOUR WAND

Now that you have your sacred wand, you can mark it with magical glyphs and symbols. Here is a spell to empower your magical tool.

You will need:

★ A candle
★ Your wand
★ A knife
★ Your phone
★ A soldering kit

THE SPELL

1. Light the candle.
2. If your wand is rough, use your knife to smooth it out, removing bark.
3. Search the internet for the magical glyphs and symbols you want to use and keep your phone around for reference. For example, you could use your astrological symbol, your ruling planet, or a pentagram.
4. Hold your wand.
5. Recite:
   "I call on the element of earth to imbue my wand and the symbols upon it with magic and activation. So may it be."
6. Begin to burn the symbols into your wand with your soldering kit.
7. Place your wand on your altar.
8. Blow out the candle.

INVESTMENT INCANTATION

Life is going pretty well in the financial department? Here is a money spell to help you choose the right investments.

You will need:

★ A candle
★ A Tarot card: the Seven of Pentacles
★ A plate
★ A coin
★ Mint

THE SPELL

1. Light the candle.
2. Place the Seven of Pentacles card in front of you.
3. Close your eyes and focus your awareness on the power of the card.
4. Envision yourself as the character contemplating the coins in the bush.
5. Connect to your question: "What will my investment be?"
6. Recite:
   "I call on the element of earth to bring me investment options. So may it be."
7. Place the card on the plate. Put the coin on top of the card.
8. Sprinkle mint on top of the card and coin.
9. Blow out the candle.

DEBT BE GONE!

Being in debt seems the norm these days. It's stressful when we can't seem to ever get on top of it. Here is a spell to help clear debt and make way for financial change.

You will need:

★ A candle
★ A pen and paper
★ String
★ Soil (in your garden or in a plant pot inside)
★ Salt
★ A coin

THE SPELL

1. Light the candle.
2. Prepare your sigil: you will be using the words: "No debt". Drop the vowels and any duplicate letters so you end up with: "N D B T". Write these letters on your piece of paper, arranging them in a creative way, and add the symbol for earth.
3. Hold your sigil and close your eyes.
4. Envision earth's energy pushing debt out of your life.
5. Recite:
   "I call on the element of earth to bind and clear this debt in my life. So may it be."
6. Bind your sigil by wrapping the string around it.
7. Dig a hole in the soil and sprinkle salt in it.
8. Put the sigil and coin in the hole and cover it with soil.
9. Blow out the candle.

BANISH YOUR FEAR
OF ANIMALS

A fear of animals can prevent us from fully enjoying life in general. Animals are teachers, and if you have a fear of this teacher, chances are they probably have an important message! Here is a spell to help you replace fear with love.

You will need:

★ A candle
★ Your phone
★ A plate
★ Salt
★ Soil

THE SPELL

1. Light the candle.
2. Search for an image of the animal you fear on your phone.
3. Close your eyes and envision yourself with the animal from the image and send it love.
4. Recite:
   "I call on the element of earth to push out my fear of [name the animal]. Replace it with love. So may it be."
5. Place the phone with the image of the animal on a plate.
6. Sprinkle salt and soil around your phone.
7. Leave it on your altar overnight.
8. Blow out the candle.

BANISH YOUR SELFIE ADDICTION

Selfies! We've all taken them. It's great to be reminded that we are here on this earth having this experience called life – and that this is what we look like. But if selfie-taking makes you feel bad, this is spell is for you.

You will need:

★ A candle
★ A pen
★ White sticker tape
★ Your phone

THE SPELL

1. Light the candle.
2. Prepare your sticker sigil: you will be using the words: "Selfie be gone" as well as your initials. Drop the vowels and any duplicate letters so you end up with: "S L F B G N". Write these letters on your white sticker tape, arranging them in a creative way, and add the symbol for earth.
3. Hold your sticker sigil in your hands and close your eyes.
4. Focus awareness on your heart opening to self-love.
5. Envision yourself free of your selfie addiction.
6. Recite:
   "I call on the element of earth to bind my selfie addiction. So may it be."
7. Stick the sigil over your phone's camera and leave it there for one day.
8. Blow out the candle.

RECONNECT WITH
LONG-LOST FAMILY

We may lose contact with family members, but family bonds go deep. Some family members may not be on social media or will have moved home. Use this spell to bring that family member back into your life.

You will need:

★ A candle
★ Two long blades of grass
★ A photo of the family member you have lost contact with
★ A plate

THE SPELL

1. Light the candle.
2. Hold the two blades of grass and close your eyes.
3. Focus your awareness on the image of the family member you wish to reconnect with.
4. Envision yourself reuniting with them.
5. Send them love.
6. Recite:
   "I call on the element of earth to reunite me with [name the person]. So may it be."
7. Twist the two blades of grass together.
8. Place the photo on the plate, and put the twisted blades of grass on top of the photo.
9. Blow out the candle.
10. Leave on your altar for as long as you need.

CAVE INCANTATION

Caves are portals. Next time you come across a cave, cast this initiation spell to dive deep into your unconscious.

You will need:

★ Access to a cave
★ An offering: nuts, seeds, herbs

THE SPELL

1. Place your offering at the entrance to the cave.
2. Close your eyes and envision yourself walking through the cave's portal.
3. Recite:

   "I call on the element of earth to initiate me to journey into the unconscious realms of the underworld. So may it be."

SPIRIT SPELLS

Spirit is the fifth element and is the bridge between the physical and the spiritual. It contains all of the four elements: air, water, fire and earth. Spirit is perfect for deeper spells of initiation, activation, summoning, evoking, invoking, connection, guides, ancestors, planets and celestial events. In each of these spirit spells, it is important to envision the energy of the spirit moving through you, contributing its power to your intentions.

CONNECT WITH YOUR SPIRIT GUIDE

Spirit guides are there to help you with your soul growth and can also be protectors and guardians. Often, they communicate through synchronicities and number sequences. Here is a spell to activate connection with your spirit guide.

You will need:

★ A candle
★ Music
★ A charcoal disc
★ A cauldron
★ Gum: dammar
★ A pen and paper
★ A crystal: amethyst
★ Tarot cards

THE SPELL

1. Light the candle.
2. Put on some soothing music.
3. Light the charcoal disc and place it in your cauldron.
4. Sprinkle the dammar gum onto the hot coal.
5. Draw the numbers 11:11 on the paper.
6. Wrap the paper around the crystal.
7. Hold the crystal sigil and close your eyes.
8. Feel the warmth and positivity of connecting to your spirit guide.
9. Bring awareness to your mind's eye.
10. Recite:

    "I call on spirit to bring connection with my spirit guide. So may it be."

11. Sit in quiet meditation.
12. Pull a Tarot card for a message from your spirit guide.
13. Place the card on your altar. Put the crystal sigil on top of it.
14. Blow out the candle.
15. Leave the sigil on your altar overnight.

CONNECT WITH YOUR HIGHER SELF

Your higher self is the version of you that is infinite, beyond ego constructs, and connected to source energy. Cast this spell to connect with your higher self, to enhance your healing, magical or creative work.

You will need:

★ A candle
★ Music
★ A charcoal disc
★ A cauldron
★ Resin: frankincense
★ A pen and paper
★ Crystals: kyanite, clear quartz
★ Tarot cards

THE SPELL

1. Light the candle.
2. Put on some soothing music.
3. Light the charcoal disc and place it in your cauldron.
4. Sprinkle the frankincense on the hot coal.
5. Prepare your sigil: you will be using the words: "Higher self". Drop the vowels and any duplicate letters so you end up with: "H G R S L F". Write these letters on your piece of paper, arranging them in a creative way, and add the symbol for spirit.
6. Wrap the paper around your crystal.
7. Hold the crystal sigil and close your eyes.
8. Recite:
   "I call on spirit to bring connection with my higher self. So may it be."
9. Pull a Tarot card for a message from your spirit guide. Place the card on your altar with the crystal sigil on top.
10. Blow out the candle.
11. Leave the card and sigil on your altar overnight.

CONNECT WITH THE SPIRIT
OF YOUR UNBORN CHILD

Many people feel a connection with the spirits of their unborn children. Some even dream of them! This spell will help you connect.

You will need:

- ★ A candle
- ★ A charcoal disc
- ★ A cauldron
- ★ Resin: copal
- ★ A pen and paper
- ★ A crystal:
  clear quartz
- ★ Tarot cards

THE SPELL

1. Prepare by finding your number. Write down your first name and the words "Baby spirit". Count the number of letters. Then add these digits together (19 letters is 1+9=10). If this provides a double digit, add the two digits again so you end with a single number.
2. Light the candle.
3. Light the charcoal disc and place it in your cauldron.
4. Sprinkle the copal on the hot coal.
5. Write your number on a piece of paper and add the symbol for spirit.
6. Wrap the paper around your crystal.
7. Hold the crystal sigil and close your eyes.
8. Recite:
   "I call on spirit to bring connection with the spirit of my unborn child. So may it be."
9. Pull a Tarot card for a message from your unborn child. Place the card on your altar with the crystal sigil on top.
10. Blow out the candle.

CONNECT WITH YOUR ANCESTORS

Our ancestors can act as guides, guardians and teachers, helping us along our life path. Honouring ancestors is integral to many cultural practices – honour yours, too, with this spell. This should be cast during the liminal thresholds of sunrise or sunset.

You will need:

★ Photos of your ancestors
★ An heirloom of your choice
★ Offerings: fruit, flowers
★ A candle
★ A charcoal disc
★ A cauldron
★ Resin: myrrh
★ Tarot cards

THE SPELL

1. Arrange the photos of your ancestors on your altar, as well as an heirloom and your offerings.
2. Light the candle.
3. Light the charcoal disc and place it in your cauldron.
4. Sprinkle myrrh on the hot coal.
5. Hold one of the heirlooms in your hand and close your eyes.
6. Connect to your heart and visualize it opening to love.
7. Recite:
   "I call on spirit to connect me to my ancestors. So may it be."
8. Sit in meditation and observe all experiences.
9. Pull a Tarot card to receive a message from your ancestors.
10. Blow out the candle.

CONNECT WITH LIGHT ORBS

Orbs of light are manifestations of spirit. They can show up in photos and videos, and a gifted few can see them with the naked eye. These orbs can serve as prompts or guides. Here is a connection spell to help activate this gift.

You will need:

★ A candle
★ Music
★ Offering: fresh flowers
★ A charcoal disc
★ A cauldron
★ Gum: dammar
★ Crystals: malachite, amazonite, turquoise, amethyst, clear quartz, angelite, jade
★ Tarot cards

THE SPELL

1. Light the candle.
2. Put on some soothing music.
3. Place your offering of fresh flowers before you.
4. Light the charcoal disc and place it in your cauldron.
5. Sprinkle dammar gum on the hot coal.
6. Create a crystal grid with your crystals.
7. Imagine yourself and the crystal grid being filled with powerful light.
8. Feel the high vibrations in your body and envision your third eye opening.
9. Visualize the orbs of light coming to you.
10. Recite:

    "I call spirit to connect me with the orbs of light. May the orbs guide me in my day-to-day journey in life. So may it be."

11. Envision the orbs of light all around you.
12. Pull a Tarot card for a guiding message.
13. Blow out the candle.

AUTOMATIC WRITING

Automatic writing is the ability to channel spirit through the act of writing. The downloads of information come through as you write the messages down on paper. This can be an incredible way to help yourself and others as you journey through life. Try this spell to activate your potential.

You will need:

★ A candle
★ A charcoal disc
★ A cauldron
★ Gum: dammar
★ A crystal: clear quartz
★ A pen
★ A jar
★ Fennel

THE SPELL

1. Light the candle.
2. Light the charcoal disc and place it in your cauldron.
3. Sprinkle dammar gum on the hot coal.
4. Hold your crystal and a pen.
5. Envision a channel above you opening up above your head.
6. Feel the high vibrations it brings to you.
7. Envision information coming through you to your fingertips.
8. Recite:
   "I call spirit to activate my automatic writing. So may it be."
9. Prepare your spell jar by adding the pen, crystal and fennel. Trap the smoke from the dammar gum in the jar and seal the lid using wax from the candle.
10. Place the spell jar on your altar.
11. Blow out the candle.

SEE AURAS

Seeing another person's aura is a beautiful experience. The first time I saw another's aura was during an 11-day silent meditation retreat. I was in the meditation hall. I sat in awe, watching the beautiful light and colours radiate from the women sitting in front of me. Seeing another person's energy can help you as a healer or practitioner – the light and colour gives us information about a person's needs or wellbeing. Here is a spell to connect you with this ability.

You will need:

★ A candle

★ A pen and paper

★ A crystal:
  aura quartz

THE SPELL

1. Light the candle.

2. Prepare your sigil: you will be using the word: "Aura". Drop the vowels and any duplicate letters, so you end up with: "R". Add the symbol for the spirit and draw an eye.

3. Wrap the paper around your crystal.

4. Hold the crystal sigil and close your eyes.

5. Envision your third eye and the crystal sigil filled with powerful light.

6. Recite:

   "I call on spirit to activate my third eye to see auras. So may it be."

7. Place your sigil on your altar.

8. Blow out the candle.

TELEKINESIS

Telekinesis is the psychic ability to move objects or effect transformation in the physical world with your mind and without physical interaction. It is a very rare gift that some people possess. If you want to activate this within yourself, cast this spell regularly and consistently.

You will need:

★ A candle
★ A pen and paper
★ Crystals: moldavite, amethyst, sodalite, lapis lazuli, labradorite, clear quartz
★ A small box
★ Any object of your choosing
★ A feather

THE SPELL

1. Light the candle.
2. Prepare your sigil: you will be using the word: "Telekinesis". Drop the vowels and any duplicate letters so you end up with: "T L K N S". Write these letters along with your initials on a piece of paper, arranging them in a creative way, and add the symbol for spirit.
3. Wrap the paper around your crystal.
4. Place your sigil crystal in the box with the chosen object and feather.
5. Close your eyes and envision your mind and crystal sigil filled with powerful light.
6. Recite:
   "I call on spirit to activate telekinesis. So may it be."
7. Place the box on your altar.
8. Blow out the candle.

CHANNELLING INITIATION

Channelling is the ability to receive downloads, messages and insights from spirit and then verbally communicate the message with your voice or in writing. Sometimes people not only speak the message but sing it, too. Here is an activation spell to have you connect with this gift.

You will need:

★ A candle
★ A charcoal disc
★ A cauldron
★ Gum: dammar
★ Herbs: fennel, red clover, mint
★ A teapot
★ Boiling water
★ A crystal: lapis lazuli

THE SPELL

1. Light the candle.
2. Light the charcoal disc and place it in your cauldron.
3. Sprinkle the dammar gum on the hot coal.
4. Add the herbs to a teapot and fill with hot water. Add the crystal and leave to steep for 20 minutes.
5. Drink your potion and feel its warmth clearing your throat chakra.
6. Close your eyes and envision a channel opening above you, allowing information and light to move down to your throat.
7. Recite:
   "I call on spirit to activate my gift of channelling. So may it be."
8. Ask your throat to reveal a sound to you and allow your throat to engage in producing this sound.
9. Blow out the candle.

PSYCHOPOMP INITIATION

A psychopomp helps the souls of the dead cross over safely to the other side and connect with ancestors or guides. Not everyone is called to do this line of work, on the thresholds of the living and the dead. If you feel the call, though, this spell is for you.

You will need:

★ A candle
★ A pen and paper
★ A charcoal disc
★ A cauldron
★ Resin: myrrh
★ Mugwort
★ A teapot
★ Boiling water

THE SPELL

1. Light the candle.
2. Prepare your sigil: you will be using the word: "Psychopomp". Drop the vowels and any duplicate letters so you end up with: "P S Y C H M". Write these letters along with your initials on a piece of paper, arranging them in a creative way, and add the symbol for spirit.
3. Light the charcoal disc and place it in your cauldron.
4. Sprinkle the myrrh on the hot coal.
5. Add the mugwort to a teapot and fill with hot water. Leave to steep for 20 minutes, then drink your potion.
6. Fold the sigil paper and hold it in your hand.
7. Close your eyes and set your intention to activate your role as psychopomp.
8. Recite:
   "I call on spirit to initiate me as a psychopomp so that I may be of service for the higher good. So may it be."
9. Place the sigil on your altar.
10. Blow out the candle.

PSYCHOMETRY INITIATION

Psychometry is the ability to receive information by holding an object. If you are already a clairvoyant, this could be another tool to add to your toolkit for the service of others.

You will need:

★ A candle
★ A pen and paper
★ A found object
★ A feather
★ Mugwort
★ A jar

THE SPELL

1. Light the candle.
2. Prepare your sigil: you will be using the word: "Psychometry". Drop the vowels and any duplicate letters so you end up with: "P S Y C H M T R". Write these letters along with your initials on a piece of paper, arranging them in a creative way, and add the symbol for spirit.
3. Fold the sigil paper and hold it in your hand.
4. Hold the found object and close your eyes.
5. Set your intention to activate psychometry.
6. Connect with your intention.
7. Recite:
   "I call on spirit to activate my psychometry so that I may be of service for the higher good. So may it be."
8. Put your sigil, the feather and mugwort in the jar.
9. Put a lid on the jar and seal it with wax from the candle.
10. Place the spell jar on your altar.
11. Blow out the candle.
12. Leave the spell jar on your altar for 30 days.

PSYCHIC TRANSFERENCE
INITIATION

Psychic transference is the ability to physically feel the emotions and ailments of others. This ability can deepen your healing practice and help others. Here is an activation spell.

You will need:

★ A candle
★ A pen and paper
★ A pebble
★ Mugwort
★ A small pouch

THE SPELL

1. Light the candle.
2. Prepare your sigil: you will be using the words: "Psychic transference". Drop the vowels and any duplicate letters so you end up with: "P S Y C H T R N F". Write these letters along with your initials on a piece of paper, arranging them in a creative way, and add the symbol for spirit.
3. Fold the paper and hold it in your hand.
4. Close your eyes and set your intention to activate psychic transference.
5. Recite:
   "I call on spirit to activate my psychic transference so that I may be of service for the higher good. So may it be."
6. Put your sigil, the pebble and the mugwort in the small pouch.
7. Blow out the candle.
8. Place the spell bag under your pillow at night and carry it around with you during the day.

MEDIUMSHIP INITIATION

A medium acts as communicators between the dead and the living. This is a beautiful gift that can bring closure and peace to the bereaved. Not everyone is called to mediumship, but if you feel that it is for you, try this activation spell.

You will need:

★ A candle
★ A pen and paper
★ A charcoal disc
★ A cauldron
★ Resin: myrrh
★ A Tarot card: Death
★ Mugwort

THE SPELL

1. Light the candle.
2. Prepare your sigil: you will be using the word: "Mediumship". Drop the vowels and any duplicate letters so you end up with: "M D S H P". Write these letters along with your initials on a piece of paper, arranging them in a creative way, and add the symbol for spirit.
3. Light the charcoal disc and place it in your cauldron.
4. Sprinkle some myrrh on the hot coal.
5. Place the Death card in front of you.
6. Fold the sigil paper and hold it in your hand.
7. Close your eyes and set your intention to activate mediumship.
8. Recite:
   "I call on spirit to activate my mediumship abilities so that I may be of service for the higher good. So may it be."
9. Place your sigil on your altar with the Death card on top and mugwort sprinkled over.
10. Blow out the candle.

PSYCHIC BOOST

As psychics, we have days where we are more attuned to the subtle signs than others. Here is a spell to boost your sensitivities before seeing a client or helping out a friend.

You will need:

★ Access to a tree
★ Your phone

THE SPELL

1. Find a tree.
2. Close your eyes and visualize putting your ego aside.
3. Envision a channel of light opening above your head.
4. Hold in your mind's eye an image of the numbers 11:11.
5. Recite:

   "I call spirit to give me a psychic boost. So may it be."
6. Envision the numbers downloading into your mind.
7. Send yourself the number "11:11".

ANIMAL TELEPATHY BOOSTER

This spell is for animal companion psychics who need a little boost before seeing a client.

You will need:

★ Access to a tree
★ Your phone

THE SPELL

1. Find a tree.
2. Close your eyes and visualize putting your ego aside.
3. Envision a channel of light opening above your head.
4. Hold in your mind's eye an image of the numbers 11:11.
5. Recite:
   "I call spirit to give me a psychic boost. So may it be."
6. Envision the numbers downloading into your mind.
7. Send yourself a digital sigil with an animal emoji and the number 11:11, like this: 11 🐨 11

GHOST BE GONE QUICK

Ghosts don't just haunt houses. They can also be sensed in public places like train stations, public toilets and pubs. Though often harmless, you may wish to remove the chilling presence. Here is a spell to cast when you are out and about and sense a ghost.

✳

You will need:
★ Your phone

THE SPELL

1. Close your eyes and envision spirit energy sending the ghost on its way.
2. Recite:
   "I call spirit to move this ghost on its way. So may it be."
3. Send yourself a digital sigil with the shooting star and ghost emojis, like this: 💫👻💫

RIP BLESSINGS

News that someone has passed away is heartbreaking but inevitable. Whether it's a person known to you or someone in the public eye, death affects us. Here is a spell to honour the deceased, send love to their next of kin and help them with the transition of their soul.

✳

You will need:
★ Your phone

THE SPELL

1. Close your eyes and envision sending light, love and peace to the deceased and their loved ones.

2. Recite:

   *"I call spirit to bring light, love and peace
   to [name of deceased] and their loved ones.
   May they rest in peace. So may it be."*

3. Send yourself a digital sigil with the
   candle and heart emojis, like this: 🕯️💜🕯️

 # BANISHING PSYCHIC
VAMPIRES

Psychic vampires are a real drain. Next time you find yourself out
and about with a psychic vampire, try this tech spell to protect your
energy and send them on their way!

You will need:

★ Your phone

THE SPELL

1. Close your eyes and envision spirit energy
   sending the psychic vampire on their way.

2. Recite:

   *"I call spirit to send this psychic vampire
   on their way. So may it be."*

3. Send yourself a digital sigil with the shooting
   star and vampire emojis, like this: 🌠🧛🌠

PAST LIFE MEMORY INITIATION

Revisiting past lives in visions, meditations or dreams can be an incredible opportunity to heal, integrate trauma and find closure. Here is an initiation spell to help you on your way.

You will need:

★ A candle
★ A charcoal disc
★ A cauldron
★ Resin: copal
★ Crystals: amethyst, clear quartz
★ Herbs: mugwort, yarrow, valerian
★ A small pouch

THE SPELL

1. Light the candle.
2. Light the charcoal disc and place it in your cauldron.
3. Sprinkle copal on the hot coal and cleanse yourself with the smoke.
4. Hold your crystal and relax into your mediation.
5. Recite:
   "I call spirit to activate access to my past lives. May I be initiated into service. So may it be."
6. Continue to meditate, travelling down a winding staircase until you come to a door. Open the door and observe what unfolds.
7. Add the crystal and herbs to the pouch.
8. Blow out the candle.
9. Keep the pouch under your pillow for seven nights, and before you go to sleep, set intentions to connect to a past life. Observe your body falling asleep but keep your mind awake.
10. When you feel a trembling in your body, will your consciousness to connect to that past life.

CONNECT WITH SATURN

Saturn is a powerful archetypal planet associated with structure, healthy boundaries and wisdom. Cast this spell when you need a quick blast of these qualities in your day.

You will need:

★ Your phone

THE SPELL

1. Close your eyes and visualize putting your ego aside.
2. Envision a channel of light opening above your head.
3. Hold in your mind's eye an image of the numbers 11:11.
4. Recite:
   "I call spirit to connect me with the energy of Saturn to help me with my day. So may it be."
5. Envision the numbers downloading into your mind.
6. Send yourself a digital sigil with the Saturn emoji and the number 11:11, like this: 11 ♄ 11

CONNECT WITH VENUS

Venus is a powerful archetypal planet associated with beauty, love, romance and the arts. Cast this spell when you need a quick blast of these qualities in your day.

You will need:

★ Your phone

THE SPELL

1. Close your eyes and visualize putting your ego aside.
2. Envision a channel of light opening above your head.
3. Hold in your mind's eye an image of the numbers 11:11.
4. Recite:

   "I call spirit to connect me with the energy of Venus to help me with my day. So may it be."
5. Envision the numbers downloading into your mind.
6. Send yourself a digital sigil with the Venus symbol and the number 11:11, like this: 11 ♀ 11

CONNECT WITH JUPITER

Jupiter is a powerful archetypal planet associated with abundance, expansion and protection. Cast this spell when you need a quick blast of these qualities in your day.

You will need:

★ Your phone

THE SPELL

1. Close your eyes and visualize putting your ego aside.
2. Envision a channel of light opening above your head.
3. Hold in your mind's eye an image of the numbers 11:11.
4. Recite:

   "I call spirit to connect me with the energy of Jupiter to help me with my day. So may it be."
5. Envision the numbers downloading into your mind.
6. Send yourself a digital sigil with the Jupiter symbol and the number 11:11, like this: 11 ♃ 11

CONNECT WITH MARS

Mars is a powerful archetypal planet associated with action, confidence and power. Cast this spell when you need a quick blast of these qualities in your day.

You will need:

★ Your phone

THE SPELL

1. Close your eyes and visualize putting your ego aside.
2. Envision a channel of light opening above your head.
3. Hold in your mind's eye an image of the numbers 11:11.
4. Recite:
   "I call spirit to connect me with the energy of Mars to help me with my day. So may it be."
5. Envision the numbers downloading into your mind.
6. Send yourself a digital sigil with the Mars symbol and the number 11:11, like this: 11 ♂ 11

CONNECT WITH MERCURY

Mercury is a powerful archetypal planet of communication, technology and innovation. Cast this spell when you need a quick blast of these qualities in your day.

You will need:

★ Your phone

THE SPELL

1. Close your eyes and visualize putting your ego aside.
2. Envision a channel of light opening above your head.
3. Hold in your mind's eye an image of the numbers 11:11.
4. Recite:

   "I call spirit to connect me with the energy of Mercury to help me with my day. So may it be."

5. Envision the numbers downloading into your mind.
6. Send yourself a digital sigil with the Mercury symbol and the number 11:11, like this: 11 ☿ 11

CONNECT WITH NEPTUNE

Neptune is a powerful archetypal planet associated with mysticism, dreams and creativity. Cast this spell when you need a quick blast of these qualities in your day.

You will need:

★ Your phone

THE SPELL

1. Close your eyes and visualize putting your ego aside.
2. Envision a channel of light opening above your head.
3. Hold in your mind's eye an image of the numbers 11:11.
4. Recite:
   "I call spirit to connect me with the energy of Neptune to help me with my day. So may it be."
5. Envision the numbers downloading into your mind.
6. Send yourself a digital sigil with the Neptune symbol and the number 11:11, like this: 11 ♆ 11

CONNECT WITH URANUS

Uranus is a powerful archetypal planet associated with revolution, innovation and community. Cast this spell when you need a quick blast of these qualities in your day.

⊕

You will need:

★ Your phone

THE SPELL

1. Close your eyes and visualize putting your ego aside.
2. Envision a channel of light opening above your head.
3. Hold in your mind's eye an image of the numbers 11:11.
4. Recite:
   "I call spirit to connect me with the energy of Uranus to help me with my day. So may it be."
5. Envision the numbers downloading into your mind.
6. Send yourself a digital sigil with the Uranus symbol and the number 11:11, like this: 11 ♅ 11

CONNECT WITH PLUTO

Pluto is a powerful archetypal planet of the shadow self, the unconscious and deep transformation. Engage in this spell on-the-go when you are ready to activate these qualities into your life. ✷

You will need:

★ Your phone

THE SPELL

1. Close your eyes and visualize putting your ego aside.
2. Envision a channel of light opening above your head.
3. Hold in your mind's eye an image of the numbers 11:11.
4. Recite:
   "I call spirit to connect me with the energy of Pluto to help me with my day. So may it be."
5. Envision the numbers downloading into your mind.
6. Send yourself a digital sigil with the Pluto symbol and the number 11:11, like this: 11 ♇ 11

CONNECT WITH ARIES

Aries is a powerful astrological sign associated with action, initiation and courage. Cast this spell when you need a quick blast of these qualities in your day.

⊛

You will need:

★ Your phone

THE SPELL

1. Close your eyes and visualize putting your ego aside.
2. Envision a channel of light opening above your head.
3. Recite:
   "I call spirit to connect me with the energy of Aries to help me with my day. So may it be."
4. Envision the energy flowing into you.
5. Send yourself a digital sigil with your initials and the Aries emoji, like this: T ♈ C

  # CONNECT WITH TAURUS

Taurus is a powerful astrological sign associated with loyalty, sensuality and pragmatism. Cast this spell when you need a quick blast of these qualities in your day.

⊛

You will need:

★ Your phone

THE SPELL

1. Close your eyes and visualize putting your ego aside.

2. Envision a channel of light opening above your head.
3. Recite:

   "I call spirit to connect me with the energy of Taurus to help me with my day. So may it be."
4. Envision the energy flowing into you.
5. Send yourself a digital sigil with your initials and the Taurus emoji, like this: T ♉ C

  # CONNECT WITH GEMINI

Gemini is a powerful astrological sign of freedom, intelligence and social interaction. Cast this spell when you need a quick blast of these qualities in your day.

You will need:
★ Your phone

THE SPELL

1. Close your eyes and envision putting your ego aside.
2. Envision a channel of light opening above your head.
3. Recite:

   "I call spirit to connect me with the energy of Gemini to help me with my day. So may it be."
4. Envision the energy flowing into you.
5. Send yourself a digital sigil with your initials and the Gemini emoji, like this: T ♊ C

CONNECT WITH CANCER

Cancer is a powerful astrological sign associated intuition, sensitivity and family. Cast this spell when you need a quick blast of these qualities in your day.

You will need:

★ Your phone

THE SPELL

1. Close your eyes and visualize putting your ego aside.
2. Envision a channel of light opening above your head.
3. Recite:
   "I call spirit to connect me with the energy of Cancer to help me with my day. So may it be."
4. Envision the energy flowing into you.
5. Send yourself a digital sigil with your initials and the Cancer emoji, like this: T ♋ C

  # CONNECT WITH LEO

Leo is a powerful astrological sign associated with extroversion, bravery and fame. Cast this spell when you need a quick blast of these qualities in your day.

You will need:

★ Your phone

THE SPELL

1. Close your eyes and visualize putting your ego aside.

2. Envision a channel of light opening above your head.
3. Recite:
   "I call spirit to connect me with the energy of Leo to help me with my day. So may it be."
4. Envision the energy flowing into you.
5. Send yourself a digital sigil with your initials and the Leo emoji, like this: T ♌ C

 ## CONNECT WITH VIRGO

Virgo is a powerful astrological sign of service, organization and perfection. Engage in this spell on the go when you need a quick blast of these qualities in your day.

You will need:
★ Your phone

THE SPELL

1. Close your eyes and envision putting your ego aside.
2. Envision a channel of light opening above your head.
3. Recite:
   "I call spirit to connect me with the energy of Virgo to help me with my day. So may it be."
4. Envision the energy flowing into you.
5. Send yourself a digital sigil with your initials and the Virgo emoji, like this: T ♍ C

CONNECT WITH LIBRA

Libra is a powerful astrological sign associated with balance, beauty and peacekeeping. Cast this spell when you need a quick blast of these qualities in your day.

You will need:

★ Your phone

THE SPELL

1. Close your eyes and visualize putting your ego aside.
2. Envision a channel of light opening above your head.
3. Recite:

   "I call spirit to connect me with the energy of Libra to help me with my day. So may it be."
4. Envision the energy flowing into you.
5. Send yourself a digital sigil with your initials and the Libra emoji, like this: T ♎ C

CONNECT WITH SCORPIO

Scorpio is a powerful astrological sign associated with magnetism, transformation and psychic ability. Cast this spell when you need a quick blast of these qualities in your day.

You will need:

★ Your phone

THE SPELL

1. Close your eyes and visualize putting your ego aside.

2. Envision a channel of light
      opening above your head.
   3. Recite:
      *"I call spirit to connect me with the energy of
      Scorpio to help me with my day. So may it be."*
   4. Envision the energy flowing into you.
   5. Send yourself a digital sigil with your initials
      and the Scorpio emoji, like this: T ♏ C

CONNECT WITH SAGITTARIUS

Sagittarius is a powerful astrological sign associated with travel,
philosophy and social activity. Cast this spell when you need a quick
blast of these qualities in your day.

You will need:

★ Your phone

THE SPELL

1. Close your eyes and visualize
   putting your ego aside.
2. Envision a channel of light
   opening above your head.
3. Recite:
   *"I call spirit to connect me with the
   energy of Sagittarius to help me
   with my day. So may it be."*
4. Envision the energy flowing into you.
5. Send yourself a digital sigil with your initials
   and the Sagittarius emoji, like this: T ♐ C

CONNECT WITH CAPRICORN

Capricorn is a powerful astrological sign associated with determination, hard work and loyalty. Cast this spell when you need a quick blast of these qualities in your day.

You will need:

★ Your phone

THE SPELL

1. Close your eyes and visualize putting your ego aside.
2. Envision a channel of light opening above your head.
3. Recite:
   "I call spirit to connect me with the energy of Capricorn to help me with my day. So may it be."
4. Envision the energy flowing into you.
5. Send yourself a digital sigil with your initials and the Capricorn emoji, like this: T ♑ C

CONNECT WITH AQUARIUS

Aquarius is a powerful astrological sign associated with technology, futurism and intelligence. Cast this spell when you need a quick blast of these qualities in your day.

You will need:

★ Your phone

THE SPELL

1. Close your eyes and visualize putting your ego aside.

2. Envision a channel of light opening above your head.

3. Recite:

   "I call spirit to connect me with the energy of Aquarius to help me with my day. So may it be."

4. Envision the energy flowing into you.

5. Send yourself a digital sigil with your initials and the Aquarius emoji, like this: T ≈ C

  # CONNECT WITH PISCES

Pisces is a powerful astrological sign associated with creativity, sensitivity and intuition. Cast this spell when you need a quick blast of these qualities in your day.

You will need:
★ Your phone

THE SPELL

1. Close your eyes and visualize putting your ego aside.

2. Envision a channel of light opening above your head.

3. Recite:

   "I call spirit to connect me with the energy of Pisces to help me with my day. So may it be."

4. Envision the energy flowing into you.

5. Send yourself a digital sigil with your initials and the Pisces emoji, like this: T ♓ C

SCRYING INITIATION

Scrying is an ancient practice of divination employing a reflective surface to receive messages and insights by way of visions. Scrying tools include obsidian scrying mirrors, black mirrors, crystal balls or bowls of water. Here is an initiation spell to get you started. While starting out, it is useful to ask your scrying tools questions at least once a week.

You will need:

★ A candle
★ A scrying tool: an obsidian mirror, black mirror, crystal ball, or bowl of water
★ A charcoal disc
★ A cauldron
★ Resin: frankincense

THE SPELL

1. Light the candle.
2. Place your scrying tool in front of you.
3. Light the charcoal disc and place it in your cauldron.
4. Sprinkle frankincense on the hot coal.
5. Relax into your meditation.
6. Envision yourself and the scrying tool emanating powerful light.
7. Envision your third eye opening and connecting to your scrying tool.
8. Cleanse your scrying tool with the smoke of the frankincense.
9. Recite:
   "I call spirit to cleanse and claim this scrying tool. May it be activated into service. So may it be."
10. Place your scrying tool on your altar.
11. Blow out the candle.

TAROT INITIATION

Tarot cards come into our lives right when we need them. A complex 78-card system of divination, it can feel daunting to learn the deck's symbolism and cryptic messages. But you will get there! Here is an initiation spell for when you first receive your deck.

You will need:

★ A candle
★ A charcoal disc
★ A cauldron
★ Resin: frankincense
★ Tarot cards

THE SPELL

1. Light the candle.
2. Light the charcoal and place it in the cauldron.
3. Sprinkle frankincense on the hot coal.
4. Spread the Tarot cards out in front of you.
5. Relax into your meditation.
6. Envision yourself and your cards being filled with powerful light.
7. Visualize your third eye opening and connecting to your cards.
8. Cleanse your cards with the smoke of the frankincense.
9. Recite:
   "I call spirit to cleanse and claim these Tarot cards. May they be activated into service. So may it be."
10. Greet each card.
11. Study each card and feel its energy.
12. Place the deck on your altar.
13. Blow out the candle.

PENDULUM INITIATION

An ancient divination tool, the pendulum can be used to answer your questions. Here is an initiation spell for when you receive your first pendulum.

✳

You will need:

★ A candle
★ A charcoal disc
★ A cauldron
★ Resin: frankincense
★ Your pendulum

How to use a pendulum:

Hold the pendulum in your hand with an outstretched arm. Think "yes" and see whether it goes clockwise or anti clockwise; think "no" and notice the direction.

THE SPELL

1. Light the candle.
2. Light the charcoal disc and place it in your cauldron.
3. Sprinkle frankincense on the hot coal.
4. Place your pendulum in front of you.
5. Relax into your meditation and envision yourself and your pendulum being filled with powerful light.
6. Visualize your third eye opening and connecting to your pendulum.
7. Cleanse your pendulum with the smoke of the frankincense.
8. Recite:
   "I call spirit to cleanse and claim this pendulum. May they be activated into service. So may it be."
9. Ask your pendulum any questions that come to mind and observe any thoughts or feelings that arrive as your answer.
10. Place your pendulum on your altar.
11. Blow out the candle.

RUNE STONES INITIATION

Runes hold power and are symbols of inherent qualities connected to magic. The symbols on the stones derive from an ancient Norse alphabet and are used for casting spells and divination. Here is an initiation spell for your new set of stones.

You will need:

- ★ A candle
- ★ A charcoal disc
- ★ A cauldron
- ★ Resin: frankincense
- ★ Your rune stones

THE SPELL

1. Light the candle.
2. Light the charcoal disc and place it in your cauldron.
3. Sprinkle frankincense on the hot coal.
4. Place your rune stones in front of you.
5. Relax into your meditation and envision yourself and your rune stones being filled with powerful light.
6. Visualize your third eye opening and connecting to your rune stones.
7. Cleanse your rune stones with the smoke of the frankincense.
8. Recite:
   "I call spirit to cleanse and claim these rune stones. May they be activated into service. So may it be."
9. Ask your rune stones any questions that come to mind. Cast your stones onto a surface and observe any thoughts or feelings that arrive.
10. Place your rune stones on your altar.
11. Blow out the candle.

PALM READING INITIATION

Palmistry has existed world-over for millennia. This art requires training, research, study and deep intuition. I recommend trying this spell after you've gained a foundational knowledge of palmistry.

You will need:

★ A candle
★ A charcoal disc
★ A cauldron
★ Resin: frankincense

THE SPELL

1. Light the candle.
2. Light the charcoal disc and place it in your cauldron.
3. Sprinkle frankincense on the hot coal.
4. Relax into your meditation and envision yourself and your hands being filled with powerful light.
5. Visualize your third eye opening and connecting to your palms.
6. Cleanse the palms of your hands with the smoke of the frankincense.
7. Recite:

   "I call spirit to cleanse and claim the palms of my hands. May my knowledge of palmistry be activated into service. So may it be."
8. Blow out the candle.

ORACLE CARDS INITIATION

Oracles cards are creative and widely varied. They are much easier to learn than a 78-card Tarot deck because they are bespoke and usually have much less cards in the system. Decks can vary from angel cards to animal cards. Find a deck that resonates with you! Here is an initiation spell for when you first receive your deck.

You will need:

★ A candle
★ A charcoal disc
★ A cauldron
★ Resin: frankincense
★ Your oracle cards

THE SPELL

1. Light the candle.
2. Light the charcoal disc and place it in your cauldron.
3. Sprinkle frankincense on the hot coal.
4. Lay the oracle cards out in front of you.
5. Relax into your meditation and envision yourself and your cards being filled with powerful light.
6. Visualize your third eye opening and connecting to your cards.
7. Cleanse your cards with the smoke of the frankincense.
8. Recite:

   "I call spirit to cleanse and claim these oracle cards. May they be activated into service. So may it be."

9. Move through each card in your deck, greeting each by saying "hello", and connecting with their energies.
10. Place the deck on your altar.
11. Blow out the candle.

OUIJA BOARD INITIATION

A ouija board aids communication with the dead and the spirit realm. Here is an initiation spell for when you receive your first board.

You will need:

- ★ A candle
- ★ A charcoal disc
- ★ A cauldron
- ★ Resins: frankincense, myrrh
- ★ Your ouija board

THE SPELL

1. Light the candle.
2. Light the charcoal disc and place it in your cauldron.
3. Sprinkle frankincense on the hot coal.
4. Place the ouija board in front of you.
5. Relax into your meditation and envision yourself and your board filling with light.
6. Visualize your third eye opening and connecting to your board.
7. Cleanse your board with the smoke of the frankincense.
8. Recite:
   "I call spirit to cleanse and claim this ouija board. May they be activated into service. So may it be."
9. Add myrrh on the hot coal and let the smoke move over your board.
10. Recite:
    "I call spirit to activate my ouija board. So may it be."
11. Ask the board questions, and observe any answer.
12. Place your board on your altar.
13. Blow out the candle.

BIBLIOMANCY INITIATION

Here is a fun divination tool for any bookworms! Bibliomancy entails using a book to tell the future, by randomly opening it and seeing what words we find on the page in front of us. You can do this with any book that inspires you. So, let's turn the page!

You will need:

★ A candle
★ A charcoal disc
★ A cauldron
★ Resin: frankincense
★ A selection of your favourite books

THE SPELL

1. Light the candle.
2. Light the charcoal disc and place it in your cauldron.
3. Sprinkle frankincense on the hot coal.
4. Place your books in front of you.
5. Relax into your mediation and envision yourself and your books being filled with powerful light.
6. Visualize your third eye opening and connecting to your books.
7. Cleanse your books with the smoke of the frankincense.
8. Recite:
   "I call spirit to cleanse and claim these books. May they be activated into service. So may it be."
9. Flip through your books, open them at random, and see where your finger lands. This is a message.
10. Place your books on your altar.
11. Blow out the candle.

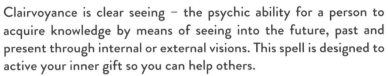

CLAIRVOYANCE INITIATION

Clairvoyance is clear seeing – the psychic ability for a person to acquire knowledge by means of seeing into the future, past and present through internal or external visions. This spell is designed to active your inner gift so you can help others.

You will need:

★ A candle
★ A charcoal disc
★ A cauldron
★ Gum: dammar
★ A crystal: azurite
★ A small pouch
★ Herbs: mugwort, yarrow

THE SPELL

1. Light the candle.
2. Light the charcoal disc and place it in your cauldron.
3. Sprinkle dammar gum on the hot coal.
4. Hold your crystal to your third eye.
5. Relax into your meditation and envision yourself being filled with powerful light.
6. Visualize your third eye opening and connecting to your gift.
7. Activate yourself with the smoke of the dammar gum.
8. Recite:
   "I call spirit to activate the gift of clairvoyance. May I be initiated into service. So may it be."
9. Place the crystal in the small bag with the herbs.
10. Blow out the candle.
11. Place the charm bag under your pillow for seven nights.

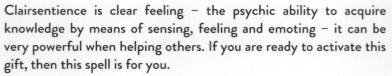

CLAIRSENTIENCE INITIATION

Clairsentience is clear feeling – the psychic ability to acquire knowledge by means of sensing, feeling and emoting – it can be very powerful when helping others. If you are ready to activate this gift, then this spell is for you.

You will need:

★ A candle
★ A charcoal disc
★ A cauldron
★ Gum: dammar
★ Herbs: mugwort, wood betony
★ Bowl of water

THE SPELL

1. Light the candle.
2. Light the charcoal disc and place it in your cauldron.
3. Sprinkle dammar gum on the hot coal.
4. Mix the herbs in the bowl of water and place it in front of you.
5. Dip your fingers in the herbal potion.
6. Relax into your meditation and envision yourself being filled with powerful light.
7. Visualize all of your senses and intuition opening and connecting to your gift.
8. Remove your hands from the herbal potion.
9. Cleanse yourself with the smoke of the dammar gum.
10. Recite:

    "I call spirit to activate the gift of clairsentience. May I be initiated into service. So may it be."

11. Blow out the candle.
12. Place the herbal potion on your altar and keep it there for seven days.

CLAIRAUDIENCE INITIATION

Clairaudience is clear hearing – the psychic ability to acquire knowledge by means of an inner hearing of words, sentences, music and conversations – it can be very powerful when helping others. If you are ready to active this gift, then this spell is for you.

You will need:

★ A candle
★ A charcoal disc
★ A cauldron
★ Gum: dammar
★ Headphones
★ Crystals: phantom quartz, clear quartz, selenite, sapphire
★ Herbs: mugwort, angelica

THE SPELL

1. Light the candle.
2. Light the charcoal disc and place it in your cauldron.
3. Sprinkle dammar gum on the hot coal.
4. Place your headphones in front of you and arrange your crystals in a grid around the them. Sit in front of the grid.
5. Relax into your meditation and envision yourself being filled with powerful light.
6. Visualize your ears opening and connecting to your gift.
7. Activate yourself with the smoke of the dammar gum.
8. Recite:

    "I call spirit to activate the gift of clairaudience. May I be initiated into service. So may it be."

9. Sprinkle the herbs around your crystal grid.
10. Blow out the candle.
11. Leave your crystal grid for seven days.

CLAIRCOGNIZANCE INITIATION

Claircognizance is clear knowing – the psychic ability to acquire knowledge without knowing how or why. This is very similar to receiving downloads. It can be very powerful when helping others. Here's a spell to explore this gift.

You will need:

★ A candle
★ A charcoal disc
★ A cauldron
★ Gum: dammar
★ A feather
★ Crystals: labradorite, amethyst, prehnite
★ Herbs: mugwort, yarrow, blue lotus

THE SPELL

1. Light the candle.
2. Light the charcoal disc and place it in your cauldron.
3. Sprinkle dammar gum on the hot coal.
4. Place your feather in front of you, and arrange your crystals in a grid around the feather. Sit in front of the grid.
5. Relax into your meditation and envision yourself being filled with powerful light.
6. Witness your mind opening and connecting to your gift.
7. Activate yourself with the smoke of the dammar gum.
8. Recite:
   "I call spirit to activate the gift of claircognizance. May I be initiated into service. So may it be."
9. Sprinkle the herbs around your crystal grid.
10. Blow out the candle.
11. Leave your crystal grid for seven days.

CLAIRGUSTANCE INITIATION

Clairgustance refers to the psychic ability to taste a flavour in your mouth related to information connected to a person. For example, you taste strawberries and discover that the person is allergic to strawberries. If you are ready to initiate this gift, this spell is for you.

You will need:

★ A candle
★ A charcoal disc
★ A cauldron
★ Gum: dammar
★ An orange
★ Crystals: chalcopyrite, blue apatite, dalmatian jasper, carnelian
★ Herbs: mugwort, yarrow

THE SPELL

1. Light the candle.
2. Light the charcoal disc and place it in your cauldron.
3. Sprinkle dammar gum on the hot coal.
4. Place an orange in front of you and arrange your crystals in a grid around the orange. Sit in front of the grid.
5. Relax into your meditation and envision yourself being filled with powerful light.
6. Visualize your tongue and palette activating, receiving your gift.
7. Activate yourself with the smoke of the dammar gum.
8. Recite:
    "I call spirit to activate the gift of clairgustance. May I be initiated into service. So may it be."
9. Sprinkle the herbs around your crystal grid.
10. Blow out the candle.
11. Leave your crystal grid for seven days.

CLAIROLFACTION INITIATION

Clairolfaction refers to the psychic ability to smell an aroma that can be connected to something specific about a person. For example, you smell burning and discover that the person survived a house fire. This spell is designed to get you in touch with this olfactory sense.

❋

You will need:

★ A candle
★ A charcoal disc
★ A cauldron
★ Gum: dammar
★ Lavender oil
★ An oil diffuser
★ Crystals: hessonite, garnet
★ Herbs: mugwort, yarrow

THE SPELL

1. Light the candle.
2. Light the charcoal disc and place it in your cauldron.
3. Sprinkle dammar gum on the hot coal.
4. Add the lavender oil to the diffuser and light it.
5. Sit in front of your oil diffuser.
6. Hold your crystal.
7. Relax into your meditation and envision yourself and the crystal being filled with powerful light.
8. Hold the crystal up to your nose and visualize your sense of smell being awakened.
9. Activate yourself with the smoke of the dammar gum.
10. Recite:

   "I call spirit to activate the gift of clairolfaction. May I be initiated into service. So may it be."

11. Blow out the candle.
12. Keep your crystal and oil diffuser on your altar for seven days.

⟨E⟩ RAINBOW INTENTION

One of the most powerful places for working with the spirit is out in nature itself. A rainbow is like spirit incarnate; it is the full spectrum of light, captured for a brief time through water droplets in the atmosphere. The next time you see a rainbow, cast this spell to strengthen your intention.

You will need:

★ A rainbow

THE SPELL

1. Spot a rainbow in the sky.
2. Close your eyes and envision the rainbow energy moving through you.
3. Connect to the magic that it brings to you.
4. Set an intention.
5. Recite:

    "I call spirit to move to me now in full rainbow colours and manifest [name intention] into my life. So may it be."

CATCH A SHOOTING STAR

Seeing a shooting star can feel surprising and joyous. If you ever get a chance to witness a shooting star, harness some of its magic with this spell.

You will need:

★ A shooting star

THE SPELL

1. Spot a shooting star in the sky.
2. Close your eyes and envision the light energy moving through you.
3. Connect to the magic that it brings to you.
4. Set an intention.
5. Recite:

   "I call spirit to move to me now through the power of this shooting star and manifest [name intention] into my life. So may it be."

HARNESS LIGHTNING

Lightning can take our breath away. Next time you witness a storm, harness some of its magic with this spell.

You will need:

★ Lightning

THE SPELL

1. Spot a lightning strike in the sky.
2. Close your eyes and envision the light energy moving through you.
3. Connect to the magic that it brings to you.
4. Set an intention.

5. Recite:

"I call spirit to move to me now through the power of this lightning strike and manifest [name intention] into my life. So may it be."

EMBODY THE SOLAR ECLIPSE

When the moon passes between earth and the sun, it obscures Earth's view of the sun. Astrologically speaking, solar eclipses are potent times to expedite or quicken any spells into manifestation. Use this spell the next time there is a solar eclipse. You can look online to see when the next one will be.

You will need:

★ A solar eclipse

THE SPELL

1. Witness the solar eclipse in the sky, but do not look directly at it!
2. Close your eyes and envision the solar energy moving through you.
3. Connect to the magic that it brings to you.
4. Set an intention.
5. Recite:

"I call spirit to move to me now through this solar eclipse to manifest [name intention] into my life. So may it be."

AURORA BOREALIS MANIFESTATION

The phenomena of the aurora borealis is like a spirit incarnate. If you ever get a chance to witness its ethereal green hues, try this spell to harness some of its beautiful and mystical light.

You will need:

★ The aurora borealis

THE SPELL

1. Look up at the aurora borealis.
2. Close your eyes and envision the light energy moving through you.
3. Connect to the magic that it brings to you.
4. Set an intention.
5. Recite:

   "I call spirit to move to me now through the light of the aurora borealis and manifest [name intention] into my life. So may it be."

 # COMET MAGIC

Comets in the night sky are powerful symbols and sometimes omens. Their mystical light can be harnessed for magical means. Try this spell if you ever get a chance to see one!

You will need:

★ A comet

THE SPELL

1. Look up at the comet in the sky.
2. Close your eyes and envision the light energy moving through you.
3. Connect to the magic that it brings to you.

4. Set an intention.

5. Recite:

   "I call spirit to move to me now through the power of this comet and manifest [name intention] into my life. So may it be."

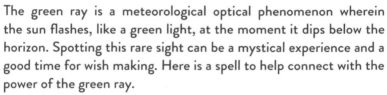

CHANNEL THE GREEN RAY

The green ray is a meteorological optical phenomenon wherein the sun flashes, like a green light, at the moment it dips below the horizon. Spotting this rare sight can be a mystical experience and a good time for wish making. Here is a spell to help connect with the power of the green ray.

You will need:

★ Green ray

THE SPELL

1. Spot the green ray on the horizon.

2. Close your eyes and envision the green ray energy moving through you.

3. Connect to the magic that it brings to you.

4. Set an intention.

5. Recite:

   "I call spirit to move to me now through the green ray to invite [name intention] into my life. So may it be."

MIRAGE MAGIC

Mirages are often otherworldly, and although easily explained through physics, they can pull you into a moment of reflection. Harness the power of this ethereal optical illusion with this spell.

You will need:

★ A mirage

THE SPELL

1. Spot a mirage on the horizon.
2. Close your eyes and envision the ethereal energy moving through you.
3. Connect to the magic that it brings to you.
4. Set an intention.
5. Recite:

   "I call spirit to move to me now through the power of this mirage and manifest [name intention] into my life. So may it be."

 # CREPUSCULAR RAYS

The appearance of crepuscular rays in the sky at twilight can feel like a spiritual awakening. This light phenomena happens when it is hazy, and the rising or setting sunlight is scattered into distinct rays. Try this spell to harness a bit of its magic!

You will need:

★ Crepuscular rays

THE SPELL

1. Spot crepuscular rays in the sky.
2. Close your eyes and envision the ethereal energy moving through you.

3. Connect to the magic that it brings to you.
4. Set an intention.
5. Recite:

   "I call spirit to move to me now through the power of these rays and manifest [name intention] into my life. So may it be."

SUN DOG

A sun dog is an atmospheric phenomenon whereby a bright spot, or halo, appears on either side of the sun. Knowing it is caused by the refraction of sunlight by ice crystals in the atmosphere doesn't make it any less magical. This spell will help you harness the power of this mystical light.

You will need:

★ A sun dog

THE SPELL

1. Spot a sun dog in the sky.
2. Close your eyes and envision the light energy moving through you.
3. Connect to the magic that it brings to you.
4. Set an intention.
5. Recite:

   "I call spirit to move to me now through the power of this sun dog and manifest [name intention] into my life. So may it be."

LUNAR ECLIPSE INTENTION

A lunar eclipse occurs when the moon moves into the Earth's shadow and in astrological terms it is a powerful time to expedite or quicken any spells into manifestation. Use this spell the next time there is a lunar eclipse. You can look online to see when the next one will be.

You will need:

★ A lunar eclipse

THE SPELL

1. Spot the lunar eclipse in the sky.
2. Close your eyes and envision the lunar energy moving through you.
3. Connect to the magic that it brings to you.
4. Set an intention.
5. Recite:

   "I call spirit to move to me now through this lunar eclipse to invite [name intention] into my life. So may it be."

DOWSING INITIATION

Here is an initiation spell for when you first receive a dowsing tool. Dowsing is a good skill to practise in nature.

You will need:

★ A candle
★ A charcoal disc
★ A cauldron
★ Resin: frankincense
★ Dowsing tool

THE SPELL

1. Light the candle.
2. Light the charcoal disc and place it in your cauldron.
3. Sprinkle frankincense on the hot coal.
4. Place your tool in front of you.
5. Relax into your meditation and envision yourself and your dowsing tool being filled with powerful light.
6. Visualize your third eye opening and connecting to your dowsing tool.
7. Cleanse your dowsing rod with the smoke of the frankincense.
8. Recite:
   "I call spirit to cleanse and claim this dowsing tool. May it be activated into service. So may it be."
9. Place your dowsing tool on your altar.
10. Blow out the candle.

CONSCIOUSNESS TIME
TRAVEL INITIATION

Travelling in time during sleep is consciousness time jumping. Here is an initiation spell to help you on your way.

You will need:

★ A candle
★ A charcoal disc
★ A cauldron
★ Resin: copal
★ Herbs: mugwort, calea zacatechichi
★ A teapot
★ Boiling water
★ An image of the era you wish to travel to
★ A crystal: lepidolite
★ A small pouch

THE SPELL

1. Light the candle.
2. Light the charcoal disc and place it in your cauldron.
3. Sprinkle copal on the hot coal.
4. Add both herbs to a teapot and fill with hot water. Leave to steep for 20 minutes.
5. Place the image of the era you wish to travel to in front of you.
6. Hold your crystal and drink your tea-potion.
7. Relax into your mediation and envision yourself and the crystal filling with light.
8. Visualize yourself entering the image.
9. Cleanse yourself with the smoke.
10. Recite:

   "I call spirit to activate consciousness time travel. May I be initiated into service. So may it be."

11. Place the image of the era, crystal and both herbs in your small pouch.
12. Blow out the candle.
13. Keep the pouch under your pillow for seven nights.

TELEPATHY INITIATION

Telepathy is the ability to transfer thoughts and communicate directly with another sentient being without exchanging words or signals. The ability can greatly enhance your work as a healer or practitioner. This spell is designed to develop your telepathy.

You will need:

★ A candle
★ A charcoal disc
★ A cauldron
★ Gum: dammar
★ A crystal: blue chalcedony
★ Herbs: mugwort, yarrow
★ A small pouch

THE SPELL

1. Light the candle.
2. Light the charcoal disc and place it in your cauldron.
3. Sprinkle dammar gum on the hot coal.
4. Hold your crystal.
5. Relax into your meditation and envision yourself and the crystal being filled with powerful light.
6. Hold the crystal up to your third eye and envision it being activated.
7. Cleanse yourself with the smoke of the dammar gum.
8. Recite:
   "I call spirit to activate the gift of telepathy. May I be initiated into service. So may it be."
9. Place your crystal in the small bag with the herbs.
10. Blow out the candle.
11. Keep charm spell bag under your pillow for seven nights.

RETROCOGNITION INITIATION

Retrocognition is the psychic ability to retrieve information from the past and deep past regarding a person or a place. This ability can greatly enhance your work as a healer or practitioner.

You will need:

★ A candle
★ A charcoal disc
★ A cauldron
★ Gum: dammar
★ Crystals: amethyst, citrine, clear quartz
★ A small pouch
★ Herbs: mugwort, yarrow

THE SPELL

1. Light the candle.
2. Light the charcoal disc and place it in your cauldron.
3. Sprinkle dammar gum on the hot coal.
4. Hold your crystal.
5. Relax into your meditation and envision yourself and the crystal being filled with powerful light.
6. Hold the crystal up to your third eye and visualize it being activated.
7. Cleanse yourself with the smoke.
8. Recite:

   "I call spirit to activate the gift of retrocognition. May I be initiated into service. So may it be."

9. Place your crystal in the small bag with the herbs.
10. Blow out the candle.
11. Keep the charm spell bag under your pillow for seven nights.

LIGHT LANGUAGE INITIATION

Light language is the unique language of your soul. It lies dormant within you waiting to be activated. Accessing this divine language comes from quietening the overthinking mind. Here is an initiation spell to help you connect to your soul language.

You will need:

★ A candle
★ A charcoal disc
★ A cauldron
★ Gum: dammar
★ Herbs: mugwort, fennel
★ A teapot
★ Boiling water
★ A crystal: lapis lazuli

THE SPELL

1. Light the candle.
2. Light the charcoal disc and place in your cauldron.
3. Sprinkle dammar gum on the hot coal.
4. Add both herbs to a teapot and fill with hot water. Leave to steep for 20 minutes.
5. Drink your tea-potion as you hold your crystal.
6. Relax into your meditation and envision yourself and the crystal being filled with powerful light.
7. Hold the crystal up to your throat and visualize your throat being activated.
8. Cleanse yourself with the smoke.
9. Recite:
   "I call spirit to activate my light language. May I be initiated into service. So may it be. "
10. Blow out the candle.

ASTRAL PROJECTION INITIATION

Astral projection has been practised for thousands of years. It occurs during sleep or meditation, when your consciousness disconnects from your body and moves freely in the astral plane. Here is an initiation spell to help you on your way.

✳

You will need:

★ A candle
★ A charcoal disc
★ A cauldron
★ Resin: copal
★ Herbs: mugwort, calea zacatechichi
★ Crystals: clear quartz, amethyst, hematite
★ A teapot
★ Boiling water
★ A small pouch
★ A feather

THE SPELL

1. Light the candle.
2. Light the charcoal disc and place it in your cauldron.
3. Sprinkle copal on the hot coal.
4. Add both herbs to a teapot and fill with hot water. Leave to steep for 20 minutes.
5. Drink your tea-potion as you hold your crystal.
6. Relax into your meditation and envision yourself and the crystal being filled with powerful light.
7. Cleanse yourself with the smoke.
8. Recite:
    "I call spirit to activate astral projection. May I be initiated into service. So may it be."
9. Place the crystal in the small bag with the feather and both herb.
10. Blow out the candle.
11. Keep the bag under your pillow.

SHAPESHIFTING INITIATION

Shapeshifting is the ancient art of transforming yourself into another sentient being. Here is an initiation spell to help you.

You will need:

- ★ A candle
- ★ A charcoal disc
- ★ A cauldron
- ★ Resin: copal
- ★ Herbs: mugwort, calea zacatechichi
- ★ A teapot
- ★ Boiling water
- ★ A crystal: lepidolite
- ★ An image of the animal you want to shapeshift into
- ★ A small pouch

THE SPELL

1. Light the candle.
2. Light the charcoal disc and place it in your cauldron.
3. Sprinkle copal on the hot coal.
4. Add both herbs to a teapot and fill with hot water. Leave to steep for 20 minutes.
5. Hold your crystal and drink the tea-potion.
6. Place the image of the animal you want to shapeshift into in front of you.
7. Relax into your meditation and envision yourself and the crystal filling with light.
8. Visualize yourself transforming.
9. Cleanse yourself with the smoke.
10. Recite:

    "I call spirit to activate shapeshifting. May I be initiated into service. So may it be."

11. Put the image, crystal and both herbs in the pouch.
12. Blow out the candle.
13. Keep the bag under your pillow for seven nights.

REMOTE VIEWING INITIATION

Remote viewing is the ability to see faraway subjects, objects, people and situations via your mind's eye. Here is an initiation spell to help you on your way.

You will need:

* A candle
* A charcoal disc
* A cauldron
* Gum: dammar
* Crystals: amethyst, celestite, labradorite, purple fluorite
* Small pouch
* Herbs: mugwort, calea zacatechichi

THE SPELL

1. Light the candle.
2. Light the charcoal disc and place in your cauldron.
3. Sprinkle dammar gum on the hot coal.
4. Hold your crystal.
5. Relax into your meditation and envision yourself and the crystal being filled with powerful light.
6. Hold the crystal up to your third eye and visualize it being activated.
7. Cleanse yourself with the smoke of the dammar gum.
8. Recite:
   "I call spirit to activate the gift of remote viewing. May I be initiated into service. So may it be."
9. Allow yourself some time to intuitively observe in meditation.
10. Place the crystal in the small bag with the herbs.
11. Blow out the candle.
12. Keep the charm bag under your pillow for seven nights.

ONEIROMANCY INITIATION

Oneiromancy is divinatory dream interpretation. Throughout human history, dream seers decoded and interpreted the dreams of tribes, communities and kingdoms and provided guidance and insight about the present and future. Here is an initiation spell to start you on your dream seer journey!

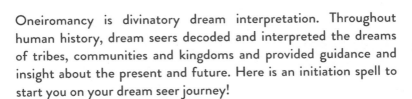

You will need:

★ A candle
★ A charcoal disc
★ A cauldron
★ Resin: copal
★ Crystals: selenite, moonstone
★ A jar
★ Herbs: mugwort, calea zacatechichi
★ Water

THE SPELL

1. Light the candle.
2. Light the charcoal disc and place it in your cauldron.
3. Sprinkle copal on the hot coal.
4. Hold your crystal.
5. Relax into your meditation and envision yourself and the crystal being filled with powerful light.
6. Visualize entering the realm of dreams.
7. Cleanse yourself with the smoke of the copal resin.
8. Recite:
   "I call spirit to activate oneiromancy. May I be initiated into service. So may it be."
9. Prepare your spell jar by adding the crystals, herbs and water.
10. Put a lid on the jar and seal it with wax from the candle.
11. Blow out the candle.
12. Keep the spell jar on your nightstand for seven nights.

YOUR MAGICAL PATH

Your magical path is a lifelong journey. As you grow and evolve in your spellcasting, you will find this work connects you more deeply to the universal forces external to you, but also within you. The more you return to the spells in this book, the more you return to yourself. Spellcraft is a true form of magical self-care and a creative process of co-creating your reality. May your spellcasting rituals continue to empower you and bring forth the life you desire to live.

ABOUT THE AUTHOR

Tree Carr is a published author and TEDx speaker who works in the esoteric realms of dreams, death and divination. A practicing witch and high priestess, Tree holds a professional certificate in Psychedelics, Altered States & Transpersonal Psychology from the Alef Trust and is a CPD Crossfields Institute Certified Death Doula.

ACKNOWLEDGEMENTS

Thank you to the amazing team at Watkins Publishing who helped to manifest this magical book. Special appreciation goes out to Ella Chappell, Brittany Willis, Elizabeth Kim, Victoria Denne, Karen Smith, Glen Wilkins, Alice Claire Coleman and Uzma Taj.

Also, a warm thank you to my agent Naz Ahsun for her guidance and helpful, pragmatic double Virgoness!